Exploring Alaska's Birds

ALASKA GEOGRAPHIC® / Volume 28, Number 1 / 2001

To teach many more to better know and more wisely use our natural resources...

EDITOR
Penny Rennick

PRODUCTION DIRECTOR
Kathy Doogan

ASSOCIATE EDITOR
Susan Beeman

MARKETING DIRECTOR
Mark Weber

ADMINISTRATIVE ASSISTANT
Melanie Britton

ISBN: 1-56661-054-0

PRICE TO NON-MEMBERS THIS ISSUE: $23.95

PRINTED IN U.S.A.

POSTMASTER:
Send address changes to:
ALASKA GEOGRAPHIC®
P.O. Box 93370
Anchorage, Alaska 99509-3370

COVER: *A semipalmated plover guards her chick. Newly hatched plovers are able to leave the nest as soon as their feathers dry. (Gary Schultz)*

PREVIOUS PAGE: *Snow geese flock overhead during migration, just one of many species that visits Alaska every year. Hundreds of thousands of migratory birds nest in the state each spring. (John W. Warden)*

FACING PAGE: *At 9 to 12 inches, the American kestrel is Alaska's smallest falcon and the only one with an obviously reddish tail and back. (James L. Davis)*

ALASKA GEOGRAPHIC® (ISSN 0361-1353) is published quarterly by The Alaska Geographic Society, 639 West International Airport Rd. #38, Anchorage, AK 99518. Periodicals postage paid at Anchorage, Alaska, and additional mailing offices. Copyright © 2001 The Alaska Geographic Society. All rights reserved. Registered trademark: Alaska Geographic, ISSN 0361-1353; key title Alaska Geographic. This issue published March 2001.

THE ALASKA GEOGRAPHIC SOCIETY is a non-profit, educational organization dedicated to improving geographic understanding of Alaska and the North, putting geography back in the classroom, and exploring new methods of teaching and learning.

MEMBERS RECEIVE *ALASKA GEOGRAPHIC*®, a high-quality, colorful quarterly that devotes each issue to monographic, in-depth coverage of a specific northern region or resource-oriented subject. Back issues are also available (see page 96). Membership is $49 ($59 to non-U.S. addresses) per year. To order or to request a free catalog of back issues, contact: Alaska Geographic Society, P.O. Box 93370, Anchorage, AK 99509-3370; phone (907) 562-0164 or toll free (888) 255-6697, fax (907) 562-0479, e-mail: akgeo@akgeo.com. A complete listing of our back issues, maps and other products can also be found on our website at **www.akgeo.com**.

SUBMITTING PHOTOGRAPHS: Those interested in submitting photos for possible publication should write or refer to our website for a list of upcoming topics or other photo needs and a copy of our editorial guidelines. We cannot be responsible for unsolicited submissions. Please note that submissions must be accompanied by sufficient postage for return by priority mail plus delivery confirmation.

CHANGE OF ADDRESS: When you move, the post office may not automatically forward your *ALASKA GEOGRAPHIC*®. To ensure continuous service, please notify us at least six weeks before moving. Send your new address and membership number or a mailing label from a recent issue of *ALASKA GEOGRAPHIC*® to: Address Change, Alaska Geographic Society, Box 93370, Anchorage, AK 99509-3370.

If your issue is returned to us by the post office because it is undeliverable, we will contact you to ask if you wish to receive a replacement for a small fee to cover the cost of additional postage to reship the issue.

COLOR SEPARATIONS: Graphic Chromatics
PRINTING: Banta Publications Group / Hart Press

ABOUT THIS ISSUE:

For their help in tracking down information and educating us on the finer points of Alaska bird lore, we'd like to thank Dr. Brina Kessel and Dan Gibson at the University of Alaska Fairbanks; Thede Tobish and Buzz Scher of Anchorage; Stan Senner and Bucky Dennerlein of the National Audubon Society, Alaska State Office; Bruce Merrell and Dan Fleming at the Z.J. Loussac Library, Anchorage; Brad Andres of the U.S. Fish and Wildlife Service; John Piatt of U.S. Geological Survey's Alaska Biological Science Center, and all the photographers who submitted such high quality photos. We looked at hundreds more excellent images than we had space to print.

For the latest information on bird sightings in the Anchorage area, call: 907-338-BIRD – Anchorage Bird Alert; or 907-235-PEEP – Homer Bird Hotline.

The Library of Congress has cataloged this serial publication as follows:

Alaska Geographic. v.1-
   [Anchorage, Alaska Geographic Society] 1972-
   v. ill. (part col.). 23 x 31 cm.
   Quarterly
   Official publication of The Alaska Geographic Society.
   Key title: Alaska geographic, ISSN 0361-1353.

   1. Alaska—Description and travel—1959-
   —Periodicals. I. Alaska Geographic Society.

F901.A266   917.98'04'505   72-92087

Library of Congress 75[79112] MARC-S.

Contents

EDITOR'S NOTE: *Science and history writer Dick Emanuel has contributed to a number of* ALASKA GEOGRAPHIC® *issues. He lives with his family in Anchorage, where they watch birds from their Hillside home.*

Citizen Scientists

Birds inhabit a special place in the human heart and imagination. Whether we are young or old, and whatever our culture, birds enchant us with flashes of color, snatches of song, and their miraculous powers of flight.

Humans have never known a sky empty of birds. Our feathered friends evolved during the Jurassic Period, at the height of the age of dinosaurs, and predated us by 150 million years.

Today, we share our planet with nearly 10,000 species of birds, from enormous, flightless ostriches, nine feet tall and weighing 350 pounds, to delicate hummingbirds, small enough to alight on the palm of a child's hand. Birds are warm-blooded, lively, often colorful, and striking to behold. Many

FACING PAGE: *Red-necked grebes build floating nests anchored to upright vegetation on Alaska's inland lakes, marshes, and ponds. Both parents care for and defend their chicks, feeding them insect larvae the first week, and later, small fish.* (Tom J. Ulrich)

Birds and People

By Richard P. Emanuel

sound elaborate calls and intricate songs, which resonate in the human heart.

Birds tantalize us, too, with their sudden appearance and disappearance. As I write, a black-capped chickadee swoops into view and alights on a branch outside my window. It shoots glances about with sharp eyes, then seemingly satisfied, chirrups a few bars of a call. An instant later, the chickadee darts off in a burst of flight I can only follow with my eyes. Where did it come from? Where is it going? What does it feel, how does it experience the world that we share?

In such encounters, for moments all too brief amid our busy days, the most common bird has the power to pull us outside of ourselves. Birds bring us scraps of nature, snippets too fleeting but nonetheless vital and nourishing to our souls. A world without birds would be a profoundly impoverished place.

○ ⬭ ◌

Ornithology, the study of birds, is unusual among modern scientific disciplines in that amateur bird-watchers can still make meaningful contributions to the field. With billions of birds spread across the planet, scientists sometimes rely on observations by amateurs to uncover and document important facts and patterns in the field.

One scientific program that solicits amateur help is Project FeederWatch, a joint effort of the National Audubon Society, the Cornell Laboratory of Ornithology, and a pair of Canadian groups.

Audubon officials and scientists at the Cornell Laboratory refer to their amateur collaborators as Citizen Scientists. In fact, some collaborators are trained scientists who participate on their own time, out of personal interest. But whether amateur or professional, Citizen Scientists

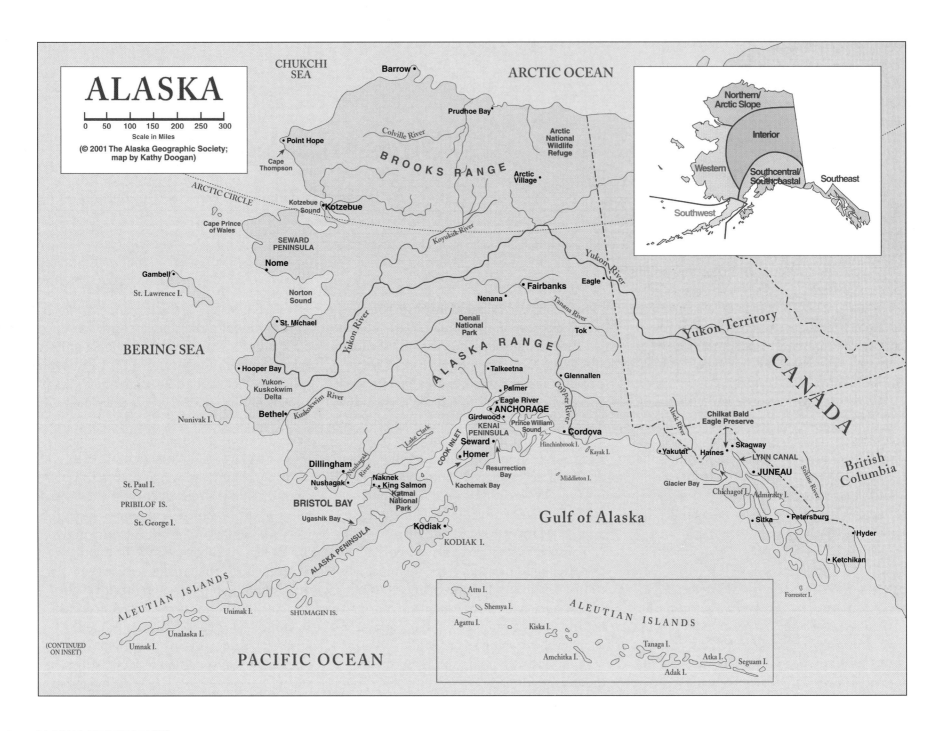

ALASKA

0 50 100 150 200 250 300
Scale in Miles

(© 2001 The Alaska Geographic Society;
map by Kathy Doogan)

CHUKCHI SEA

ARCTIC OCEAN

Barrow

Prudhoe Bay

Colville River

Arctic National Wildlife Refuge

Point Hope

Cape Thompson

B R O O K S   R A N G E

Arctic Village

ARCTIC CIRCLE

Kotzebue Sound

Kotzebue

Cape Prince of Wales

SEWARD PENINSULA

Koyukuk River

Yukon River

Gambell

Nome

Norton Sound

St. Lawrence I.

Fairbanks

Eagle

Nenana

Tanana River

BERING SEA

St. Michael

Yukon River

Denali National Park

A L A S K A   R A N G E

Tok

Yukon Territory

CANADA

Hooper Bay

Yukon-Kuskokwim Delta

Talkeetna

Glennallen

Copper River

Bethel

Kuskokwim River

Palmer

Eagle River

ANCHORAGE

Girdwood

KENAI PENINSULA

Prince William Sound

Cordova

Alsek River

Chilkat Bald Eagle Preserve

Nunivak I.

Lake Clark

COOK INLET

Seward

Homer

Hinchinbrook I.

Kayak I.

Yakutat

Haines

Skagway

LYNN CANAL

JUNEAU

British Columbia

Stikine River

Resurrection Bay

Middleton I.

Glacier Bay

Dillingham

Nushagak River

Kachemak Bay

Chichagof I.

Admiralty I.

St. Paul I.

Nushagak

Naknek

King Salmon

Katmai National Park

Gulf of Alaska

Sitka

Petersburg

PRIBILOF IS.

St. George I.

BRISTOL BAY

Ugashik Bay

Kodiak

Hyder

ALASKA PENINSULA

KODIAK I.

ALEUTIAN ISLANDS

Ketchikan

Unimak I.

SHUMAGIN IS.

Forrester I.

(CONTINUED ON INSET)

Unalaska I.

Umnak I.

PACIFIC OCEAN

Attu I.

Shemya I.

A L E U T I A N   I S L A N D S

Agattu I.

Kiska I.

Tanaga I.

Atka I.

Amchitka I.

Seguam I.

Adak I.

Northern/Arctic Slope

Interior

Western

Southcentral/Southcoastal

Southeast

Southwest

often find their studies rewarding.

An even larger citizens' effort is the annual Audubon Christmas Bird Count, or CBC. Each year around Christmas, birders fan out across North America to observe and record every individual bird and bird species found within a designated area during a 24-hour period.

The first Christmas Bird Count took place on Christmas Day, 1900, and counts have been held every year since then. The CBC has grown to be the largest and longest-running wildlife survey in history. More than 45,000 volunteers now participate each year, in some 1,700 counts in 50 states and every Canadian province. Recently, counts have been added in the Caribbean and at Central and South American sites where North American breeding birds winter.

The 1900 Christmas Bird Count was organized by ornithologist Frank Chapman in response to a holiday custom of the period called the "side hunt." Teams of hunters set out to shoot as many birds and small animals as they could in a single day, with the "victory" going to the side that bagged the most. To protest the side hunt, Chapman organized 27 friends in 25 locations to venture afield and count birds, rather than shoot them. The practice has been refined over the years and has been relatively standardized since the 1940s. Each count now canvasses a well-defined circle 15 miles in diameter. Most counts

are conducted by collegial groups.

The first Audubon Christmas Bird Count in Alaska took place in Anchorage, in 1941. The second took place in 1959, also in Anchorage, and Alaska counts have been held every year since.

The Watching Multitude

When it comes to birding enthusiasts, those who contribute to Audubon Christmas Bird Counts or to Project FeederWatch are no more than the slender tip of an enormous iceberg. Bird-watching is one of the most popular nature activities in North America. It engages tens of millions of people at various levels, from preschoolers to nursing home residents.

It is difficult to precisely estimate how many people watch birds. One complication

ABOVE LEFT: *The yellow warbler has the largest range of all wood warblers, nesting from the Atlantic to the Pacific and northern Canada and Alaska to Mexico. Weighing only about one-third of an ounce,* Dendroica petechia *can easily perch atop its favorite small shrubs. (Tom Soucek)*

ABOVE: *Through Project FeederWatch, a national cooperative effort among bird enthusiasts, tidbits of information gathered around the country are compiled into a broader understanding of bird populations and migration patterns. Here, a boreal chickadee visits a hanging feeder filled with suet that provides a high-calorie diet for birds wintering in Alaska's cold interior. (Tom Walker)*

Fresh from an old goshawk nest near Tok, in eastern Alaska, great gray owls sit quietly as researcher Ron Clarke tests the species' reputation as tame birds of prey. Rather than build their own nest, great gray owls take advantage of those left behind by hawks or eagles. Chicks begin exploring near the nest site three to four weeks after hatching. (David Roseneau)

is the wide range of knowledge and enthusiasm among birders. Some avid birders keep their eyes on feeders and neighborhood hotspots daily, and devote vacation travel to birding festivals and special locations. More casual birders are far more numerous. But across the spectrum, there are indications that the number of American birders is soaring. Membership in the American Birding Association, for example, doubled during the 1990s, from roughly 10,000 to 20,000.

A 1985 study found that a quarter of all Americans could be considered birders, and that around 10 percent watch birds at least 20 days a year. Nationwide, birders may number close to 70 million, of whom 25 million to 30 million are reasonably active.

Another indication of interest in birds might be membership in the National Audubon Society, one of the world's oldest and largest environmental organizations. The society, formed in 1886, was named for nineteenth-century ornithologist and wildlife artist John James Audubon. The 550,000-member national organization is devoted to many issues, but a prime focus of many of the group's 500 local chapters is birding.

Estimates of the amount of money spent on birding are also problematic, but the economic impact of bird-watching is undoubtedly significant. Birders buy books, binoculars, cameras and film, birdhouses, feeders, and seed. They buy outdoor clothing and many spend money on travel.

A 1991 survey of members of the American Birding Association showed that the group's members spent an average of $3,400 a year on their hobby. About 70 percent went for travel. If members' expenditures have kept pace with inflation, their average investment in birding may be $4,000 a year, for a total of $80 million spent annually by ABA birders alone. A U.S. Department of Interior study suggests that the total impact of birding may be an astonishing $15 billion to $20 billion a year.

One indication of the impact of birding

is the growing popularity of bird-watching festivals. In a directory for the year 2000, the ABA lists some 200 festivals. Events are usually co-sponsored by local businesses and chambers of commerce, often in conjunction with nearby wildlife refuges. Bethel, in western Alaska, has a fledgling bird-watching program that encourages visitors to bird the immense wetlands of the Yukon Delta refuge. Festivals typically have twin goals of fostering public education and appreciation of birds while attracting tourism, sometimes during non-peak tourist periods in spring or fall.

Three major birding festivals draw visitors to Haines, Cordova, and Homer. The attraction in Haines is the world's greatest annual gathering of American bald eagles. In the Chilkat River north of Haines, warm spring-water discharged through the streambed keeps much of the lower river ice-free and open well into winter. The Chilkat also hosts a late run of spawning salmon, and from time immemorial, the combination of salmon and open leads has attracted eagles each year, from late October into January.

At the peak, in mid-November, upwards

A white-phase gyrfalcon soars low to the ground in search of prey, most often ptarmigan, but also other birds and small mammals. Gyrfalcons weigh two to four and one-half pounds, with the female slightly larger than the male. (John Hyde)

of 3,000 eagles are drawn to the feast from hundreds of miles around. A dozen of the raptors may be seen perched in a single tree, surveying the wintry scene.

To protect the age-old conclave, Alaska created the Chilkat Bald Eagle Preserve in

Thousands of western sandpipers congregate on the Stikine River Delta each spring and fall as part of their yearly migration to and from Alaska along the Pacific Flyway. (Don Cornelius)

1982. The non-profit American Bald Eagle Foundation was born in Haines a few years later. In 1994, the group opened a building with foundation offices and a museum. Shortly thereafter, the Haines Bald Eagle Festival was hatched. The event takes place the second week of November each year.

"We have always had photographers and videographers in the fall to photograph the eagles, but not many other people knew about it," explains Dave Olerud, the Bald Eagle Foundation's founder. "We wanted to bring people in and show them this wonderful natural occurrence. It's also a great way to bring people to Haines during November, when things are a little slow."

The bald eagle festival includes daily trips to the Preserve to view the birds and other wildlife, along with scientific talks and social events around town in the evenings. The local Chilkat Native Dancers perform, and rehabilitated birds from the Bird Treatment and Learning Center, in Anchorage, are released.

"The Chilkat Natives here have two clans, the Eagle and Raven clans," Olerud says. "For an eagle to be released, it must be released by a member of the Raven clan, and vice versa. So we try to have both eagles and ravens, so that both clans can participate."

Around 400 people witness the release of rehabilitated birds, perhaps the highlight of the annual festival, Olerud says. On hand are perhaps 300 visitors from out of town. In the past, student groups from Juneau, Redmond, Wash., and as far away as Detroit and Kansas City have traveled to Haines for the festival.

In spring, shorebirds by the millions migrate to Alaska from around the world, and a pair of festivals in Southcentral Alaska has grown up to welcome them. Around the first weekend in May is the Copper River Delta Shorebird Festival, in Cordova, on Prince William Sound. First celebrated in 1990, the festival boasts the greatest number of birds of any Alaska event.

"The Copper River Delta is a large wetland, and as birds come up from the south, it's the first major wetland they find," explains Scott Novak, director of the Cordova Chamber of Commerce, a festival sponsor. "So almost every shorebird coming up from the south stops here for rest and food. The Copper River Delta is among the most significant shorebird areas in the Western Hemisphere."

An estimated 14 million shorebirds use the delta each year, including seven million western sandpipers, and five million dunlins — the entire western Alaska breeding population. During a single day in 1993, some 1.2 million birds were observed along 75 miles of Copper River Delta habitat.

Many shorebirds utilize outer barrier beaches, which are accessible only by boat or plane. But there are spots accessible by road from Cordova that afford good birding, especially at high tide. Common shorebirds include greater and lesser yellowlegs; black-bellied and American golden-plovers; spotted, least, and pectoral sandpipers; short-billed and long-billed dowitchers; whimbrels, surfbirds, sanderlings, snipes, and red-necked phalaropes.

Despite the variety and astonishing number of birds on the Copper River Delta, the Cordova event remains the smallest of Alaska's three major birding festivals. Novak estimates around 50 out-of-town visitors attend the event, which includes workshops, field trips, and a banquet in addition to the release of rehabilitated birds. Cordova's remoteness — it is unconnected to the state's road system — may explain the limited attendance, but these factors can be viewed as added attractions, Novak points out.

"It's not as crowded as other festivals," he says. "We have all of the birds and none of the people."

A week after the Cordova festival, the Kachemak Bay Shorebird Festival takes place in Homer. By the second weekend in May, some of the birds on the Copper River Delta have replenished their reserves and continued westward to the mudflats

The red-breasted nuthatch is the only species from the nuthatch family found in Alaska and, according to recent reports by FeederWatch participants in Fairbanks, seems to be expanding its territory to include more of the Interior. This male perches momentarily with a sunflower seed in Eagle River, near Anchorage. Fond also of conifer seeds and insects, it wedges its food into a tree crack or underneath bark edges, then breaks off bite-size pieces. (Roy Corral)

and wetlands around Kachemak Bay.

More than 100,000 shorebirds migrate through the bay, a fraction of the Copper River Delta shorebirds but an impressive number all the same. The variety of birds is also notable: More than 100 species have been seen in one day during Homer's festival, which began in 1993.

Birds in attendance include Aleutian terns, red-faced cormorants, Kittlitz's

To create a better understanding of migrating passerines, scientist Heidi Rubar records data on a male Wilson's warbler in Denali National Park. In the early part of the twentieth century, people killed birds to study them, but now, with new methods and improved technology, birds are captured, handled with care during observation, and released. (Patrick J. Endres)

murrelets, and Eurasian wigeons. Common shorebirds include semipalmated, western, and least sandpipers; dunlins; short-billed dowitchers; red-necked phalaropes; three species of godwits, and four species of plovers.

Homer is a five-hour drive from Anchorage and enjoys amenities commensurate with the town's status as a summer tourist destination. It is also headquarters of the sprawling Alaska Maritime National Wildlife Refuge, which is a sponsor of the Kachemak Bay Shorebird Festival.

"The festival has an important educational role, and at the same time, it expands the visitor season here," festival coordinator Dorle Scholz says. "We try to get top birding experts nationwide and even worldwide, so the quality of speakers is pretty high."

The keynote address is one of the festival's best attended events, and it typically draws more than 350 people. About a third of the attendees are local and another third are from Anchorage, but as many as

40 visitors come from outside of Alaska.

The success of the festival is important for a number of reasons, according to Scholz. For one thing, it builds local support for protecting shorebird habitat.

Scholz admits that shorebirds don't initially excite the public the way that eagles do, "but they still play an important role. So we want to get the word out about shorebirds, and about the mudflats and the wetlands. They don't look appealing, maybe, but they're a very important habitat. We want to give businesses a reason not to develop those lands, because they'll benefit from the shorebird festival."

Birding on the Edges

For anyone interested in the wide range of North American birds, Alaska is one of the continent's most exciting places. That includes Thede Tobish, a past president of the Anchorage Audubon chapter and one of the state's top birders.

"For hardcore birders who are interested in their North American list, there are obligatory places you go," Tobish explains.

Ellie Mather records data as wildlife veterinarian Dan Mulcahy performs surgery on a harlequin duck during a study of the species in Prince William Sound in 1998. Research done since the 1989 Exxon Valdez *oil spill there has confirmed harlequin populations in the area are still plagued by effects of the disaster. (Patrick J. Endres)*

"Southeast Arizona, south Texas, south Florida, and Alaska — those are the big ones."

It is no coincidence that the spots on Tobish's must-see list are all on the margins of the United States. Floridians might well see birds common around the Caribbean and in Central and South America, while Mexican birds often drift north into Texas and Arizona. Alaska, in northwestern North America, is home to boreal or far-northern species seldom seen elsewhere in the United States, along with birds ordinarily found in Asia.

Tobish began watching birds with his father, in eastern Pennsylvania. "He was mainly interested in spring warblers and he just passed it on," he says.

In 1973, Tobish moved to Alaska to attend college. Soon, his interest in birds grew to the verge of obsession. "In the 1970s, Alaska was very much a pioneering place for studies of bird status and distribution," Tobish recalls. "It still is. The size,

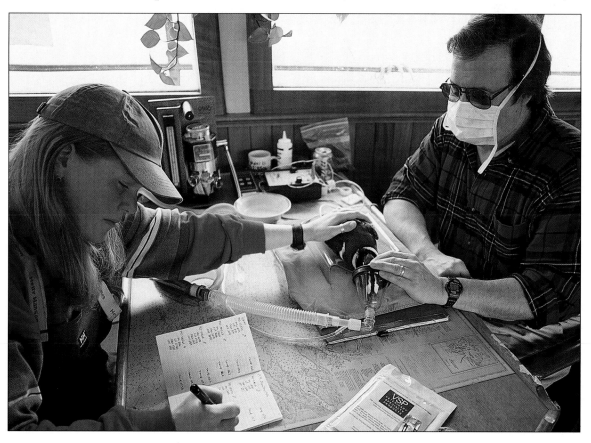

the remoteness and difficulty of access, historic knowledge [of birds] was very limited. So it got very exciting, very quickly. Even today, anywhere you go in Alaska, you have a chance to uncover something new and distinct."

While Alaska as a whole lies on the edge of the continent, Tobish's interests carry him to the edges of Alaska. His favorite birding spots are Hyder, on the Canadian border northeast of Ketchikan;

Attu, in the Aleutian Islands; and Middleton Island, in the Gulf of Alaska.

"I like to think I was instrumental in elucidating the importance of Middleton Island for bird migration," Tobish says. The island, 19 miles long by 4 miles wide, lies some 80 miles south-southwest of Cordova. A lonely rock in the stormy Gulf of Alaska, the island is little visited except by military and government workers maintaining communication and navigation gear. Since

the 1970s, biologist have conducted field research there.

"Middleton is a remote island and so it's a concentration point for migrating birds,"

BELOW LEFT: *A scientist from the Alaska Bird Observatory at Creamer's Field Migratory Waterfowl Refuge in Fairbanks blows on feathers of a savannah sparrow to check its brood sac.* Passerculus sandwichensis *typically lays four to five greenish-blue or dingy white, speckled or blotchy eggs in a ground nest of grasses. (Patrick J. Endres)*

BELOW: *Hermit thrush eggs need only 12 days of incubation. After another 12 days,* Catharus guttatus *can fly, and has a habit of slightly raising and lowering its tail just after alighting. Hermit thrushes are common along Alaska's southern coastal areas during spring, summer, and fall. (Chlaus Lotscher)*

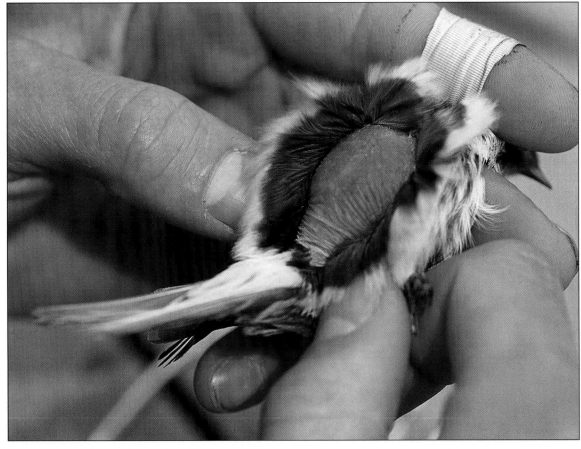

Nesting primarily on the Yukon-Kuskokwim Delta, emperor geese then fly south to winter in the Aleutian Islands. In flight, emperor geese show a proportionately shorter neck than do other goose species found in Alaska. (Lon E. Lauber)

Tobish notes. "And because it's an island, you can actually cover the habitat and find the birds that are there. You can easily survey and find the full breadth of species migrating up the Gulf Coast. Since our first trip there, in 1981, several species have been added to the state list [of birds identified in Alaska], and our overall knowledge of bird migration — fall migration, especially — has greatly increased."

There are no commercial plane flights to Middleton Island but it does have an airstrip, and charter flights are possible.

"As far as birders go, it's a kind of fantasy island," Tobish continues. "The west side is a terraced bluff with salmonberry and willow thickets. They [the habitats] concentrate the passerines [or songbirds] and we've seen some incredible birds: Nashville warblers, black-headed grosbeak, dusky warbler. We've found rarities from Asia and others from North America that aren't generally seen elsewhere in Alaska. It's also neat because you can sit on the northwest point and see seabirds very close up."

Also special to Tobish is Attu, westernmost of the Aleutian Islands. As the island in the chain that lies closest to Asia, many Asian birds are found on Attu. Even the island's flora has Asian affinities.

Tobish helped pioneer birding expeditions to the island for Attour, an ecotourism company that specializes in Alaska birding opportunities. Unfortunately, difficulty in arranging transportation and landing access and in maintaining the buildings prompted owner Larry Balch to suspend the Attu tours in fall 2000.

"My first trip to Attu was in 1977," Tobish recalls. "I led tours there for 14 years. We had numerous first records for North America. We discovered a pair of white-tailed eagles in their nest — the first pair nesting in North America."

David Sonneborn also led birding tours of Attu. An Anchorage cardiologist by profession, Sonneborn has been to the island many times.

"We had up to 80 people for tours of one, two, three, or four weeks," he says.

Intertidal zones are preferred habitat for the black oystercatcher as it feeds on mussels, clams, chitons, limpets, barnacles, and other invertebrates. Immature black oystercatchers are browner than adults and have an orange, rather than red, beak. (Tom Walker)

"A typical birder was in his late 50s, a successful businessman interested in seeing how many birds he could see in the U.S. But really, there was a variety of people. Some people would save for years to go to Attu."

Attu is 37 miles long, but easy access is limited to the island's southeast corner, where visitors used bicycles and four-wheeled all-terrain vehicles to get around.

"We'd bicycle down old roads along the shore," Sonneborn says. "Attu is so beautiful, pretty country, wonderful sunsets."

Asian migrants, such as the Terek sandpiper, Far Eastern curlew, rufous-necked stint, and Siberian rubythroat were sighted.

Other parts of Alaska are also popular with avid birders. Tours to the Kenai Peninsula and Denali National Park net resident boreal species generally new to non-Alaskans. The Pribilof Islands, St. Lawrence Island, and Nome — all on the Bering Sea — attract hundreds of birders. Barrow, Alaska's northernmost community, likewise draws many tourists, including birders.

Not all birders making these pilgrimages are from outside the state. Alaskans, too, journey in search of *rara avis*. Anchorage birder and president of the local Audubon chapter George Matz recalls a trip he made to Gambell, on St. Lawrence Island. With him were several fellow Alaska birders.

"They get lots of Eurasian birds because, well, when you're in Gambell, you can see Siberia on a clear day," Matz says. "There were seven or eight of us from Anchorage, just Alaskans making a trip in Alaska. When we got there, I counted 60 birders in Gambell. The people-watching was as good as the bird-watching, sometimes."

There were 20 or 30 spotting scopes set up along the beach. "And some of these top-notch birders were really good," Matz says. "There'd be a bird flying along way out there and they'd say, 'Oh, there's an arctic loon.' Man! I was there two days before I felt comfortable telling the difference between an arctic and a Pacific loon. There'd be a dot approaching and they could already tell."

Baby woodpeckers are altricial, meaning blind and naked at hatching, but by about four weeks, are able to eat whole insects. Here, a male three-toed woodpecker, distinguished from the female by his yellow cap, feeds a chick. Typical of woodpeckers, he props his tail against the tree for support while his toes grip the bark. Immatures have some yellow in the crown, which disappears in adult females. (Tom J. Ulrich)

Back to the Wild

By Susan Beeman, Associate Editor

Hundreds of sick, injured, and orphaned birds pass through Alaska's bird rehabilitation centers every year. Ailments run the gamut from diseases like pox and salmonella to bullet wounds, poisoning, and electrocution from power lines. Birds get hit by cars, fly into windows, and are attacked by other animals. They all have one thing in common — people have found them and want to help.

Rehabilitators stress the importance of observing an apparently abandoned, injured, or sick bird before taking any steps to "rescue" it. It might not need treatment, but if it does, that's where the centers come in, with veterinarians and expert volunteers available to answer questions and take appropriate action.

A few wild bird rehabilitation centers operate in Alaska, while several additional individuals and veterinary clinics licensed to treat wild birds fill the gaps. Centers in Juneau, Sitka, Seward, and Anchorage use trained volunteers to help restore their avian patients' health enough to release them back into the wild. Educating the public about wild birds and wild bird habitats is also a priority.

"Thirty-one common ravens, 27 bald eagles, 12 pine siskins, eight varied thrushes, one pine grosbeak, one rufous hummingbird …" the list is long for the The Juneau Raptor Center, where volunteers treated more than 200 birds in 1999. JRC President Sandy Harbanuk says, "Some people have a strong sense of obligation to help wild critters as a response to human impacts on the environment," and that's exactly what all the volunteers there do, from fund-raising to cleaning cages. The community, too, is invited to attend and celebrate releases back to the wild.

Releasing rehabilitated birds back to the wild can be emotional and tense for all involved. Volunteers sometimes become attached to their injured patients, yet know these creatures are better off returning to their natural environment. (Roy Corral)

The Alaska Raptor Rehabilitation Center in Sitka borders Tongass National Forest, prime habitat for bald eagles. The center admits mainly bald eagles to its hospital, though other birds are occasionally treated. ARRC was formed in 1980 by a group of volunteers and is now staffed by a few paid positions and many volunteers. Their goal is to release all patients back into the wild, but a handful of birds, even when healed, would not survive if released. They are kept as "education" birds, taken to schools and community gatherings to teach people the importance of learning about bird life. Face to face with a live bald eagle, the bird's wings unfolded to a span of over six feet, a child from an inner city school outside Alaska who's never seen a bird of prey up close might suddenly become interested in knowing more about the wild

places these raptors inhabit. Birds kept for education also help "tutor" young birds of the same species so the immature birds don't imprint on humans. Thousands of visitors per year attend talks and demonstrations at ARRC.

Seabird research at Seward's Alaska SeaLife Center includes rehabilitation. A project featuring pigeon guillemots, hit hard by the 1989 *Exxon Valdez* oil spill in Prince William Sound, is underway to re-establish a breeding population, an attempt to jumpstart the species in that area again.

Farther north, in Anchorage, volunteers at the Bird Treatment and Learning Center also care for Alaska's sick and injured wild birds.

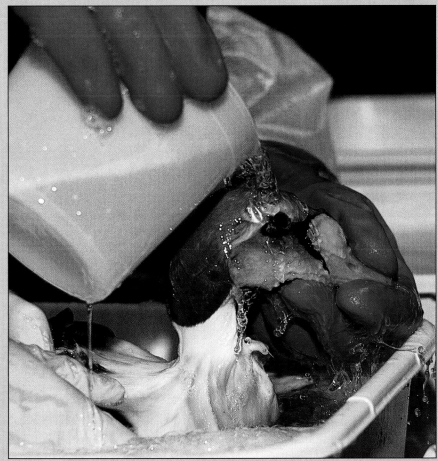

Their goal, like ARRC's and JRC's, is to release back to the wild the many species they rehabilitate, from bald eagles with eagle pox to black-capped chickadees with broken wings. Bird TLC sees ravens and hawks, owls and geese — more than 1,000 birds each year. Many are rehabilitated and released, some have sustained injuries too severe to treat and must be euthanized, and a few do not recuperate sufficiently to be set free; they are trained as education birds. With permits from the U.S. Fish and Wildlife Service and the Alaska Department of Fish and Game, Bird TLC is allowed to treat all

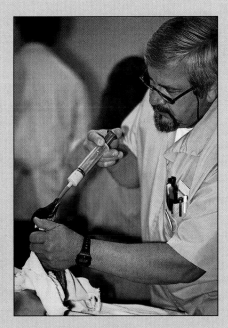

types of birds. The staff is largely composed of trained volunteers who do everything from administering medication to birds to scrubbing and disinfecting the various mats and dishes used for feeding. Dr. James R. Scott, the Anchorage veterinarian who started Bird TLC in 1988 and is now the center's medical director, performs major surgeries when needed and serves as a wellspring of knowledge for rehab volunteers.

Since most wild bird injuries occurring in urban areas are human-related, from intentional, illegal shootings to accidental collisions with cars, it makes sense that humans expend effort and funding to treat these avian victims. •

FAR LEFT: *A king eider is bathed after falling victim to a mysterious oil spill off the coast of the Pribilof Islands in the late 1990s. Most birds brought in for treatment at rehabilitation centers have been injured or sickened by some form of human contact. (Harry M. Walker)*

LEFT: *Dr. Jim Scott of the Bird Treatment and Learning Center in Anchorage cares for a Canada goose. Bird TLC treats more than 1,000 birds annually. (Roy Corral)*

LEFT: *What was once a privately owned dairy in Fairbanks is now home to a bird observatory and refuge. Canada geese, shown here, along with pintails, golden-plovers, sandhill cranes, shovelers, and mallards all visit the 1,800 acres of woods, wetlands, and fields each summer. Other species, including chickadees, redpolls, ravens, and owls are year-round residents. (Gary Schultz)*

ABOVE: *Not all human-bird interaction is positive. This common murre was found dead on the coast of Cape Thompson, northwest Alaska, with plastic "six-pack" container rings tangled around one wing, its neck and head, and through the gap in its beak, preventing the seabird from flying or eating. (David Roseneau)*

For the Birds

Veterinarian Jim Scott is a burly man of 68 who walks with a gait that betrays the repeated surgery he has suffered on both his knees. By rights, he should be nearing retirement. But it's hard to imagine the Bird Treatment and Learning Center, in Anchorage — Scott's rehabilitation facility for wild birds — without its founder and medical director.

Scott has been an Anchorage veterinarian for more than 35 years, but he grew up in Estes Park, Colo. It was an injured English sparrow which he found in a granary on his parents' land — his first patient — which put young Scott on the long path to the Bird TLC.

"Birds were always flying into the granary, attracted by the grain," Scott remembers. When he was six years old, he discovered a frightened bird with an injured wing in the building. He showed it to his mother.

"Mom said, 'You're going to have to splint this wing,' so she got a bandage. She showed me how to splint it and wrap it so the wing would be held to the body in the right position. After about 10 days, we took the wrap off and it looked fine to me. We took it outside and I held it in my hands and when I opened the top hand, why, it sat there looking at me for a minute before it flew away."

Scott pauses. "It was an important happening in a life," he says. "You wouldn't think something that small could have such a prominent position in all of life's events. But it does with me."

When he reached high school, Scott had grown to be an all-state football player, but he struggled to read at a fifth-grade level. He earned A's in geometry but he just couldn't master classes that required reading. They often ended in D's, or worse.

The problem was dyslexia, a learning disability almost unrecognized in 1950. Rebelling against the well-intentioned but hurtful advice of his principal, Scott tried college after graduation, but his reading problems proved too much. He soon left college and joined the Navy.

"In the Navy, there were a lot of difficult times," Scott recalls. "But every time I ran up against a wall I would think of that little bird, and all that it went through to get back in the air. That little bird would come to the front of my mind. It was almost like an animal spirit that would encourage me. That may sound weird, but I'm part Cherokee so animal spirits are in my realm."

In the Navy, Scott ran into a chief who was also dyslexic. "Well, he'd learned that he could take an acetate sheet that was yellow and put it over a page and all the words would unscramble," Scott says. "He was way

BELOW: *Two cliff swallows duel over a mudhole as they gather mud in their beaks for nests. Birders read the yearly return of swallows as a sure sign of spring. (Hugh Rose)*

RIGHT: *Potter Marsh, part of the Anchorage Coastal Wildlife Refuge just south of the city along the Seward Highway, sustains several species of waterfowl each summer. Mallards, one type of waterfowl that takes advantage of the marsh's ponds and grasses, let their chicks dry after hatching, then lead them directly to water. (Loren Taft/Alaskan Images)*

With tail spread and red eye combs erect, this spruce grouse struts for a potential mate. He'll announce his presence to other males in the territory by loudly whirring or snapping his wings. (Patrick J. Endres)

then westerns, then I read classics," Scott says. " And when I got out, I went to college. And it was only because of the insight of that man with the acetate sheets — and with this little bird."

After veterinary school, Scott came to Alaska to begin a practice. One day, someone brought a great gray owl that had been hit by a car into his clinic. "So I treated it," Scott says. "Pretty soon word got around and people started bringing birds to me. I've been taking care of wild birds for more than 35 years."

Scott's pro bono work on birds gradually grew until it threatened to engulf his veterinary clinic. In 1988, he formed the non-profit Bird Treatment and Learning Center. The following year, when the *Exxon Valdez* ran aground in Prince William Sound, Bird TLC geared up to rehabilitate some of the oiled birds. Many of the most seriously hurt birds were sent to Scott, in Anchorage, including two dozen eagles. Eleven of the eagles survived.

"It was kind of a M*A*S*H operation," Scott says. "We had to triage the birds," decide which ones to treat first and which ones couldn't be saved.

ahead of his time, he had just discovered this on his own."

Like the chief, Scott had a form of dyslexia that responded to color overlays. The men experimented and found that a combination of pink and yellow did the trick for the young sailor.

"So I had four years in the Navy, and with the use of those acetates and those kinds of things, I started reading comics,

Alaska's Auklets

Auklets are members of the alcid family of seabirds. Like all alcids, they use their short, pointed wings to "fly" underwater while feeding on fish and marine invertebrates. The six different species occur in various regions of Alaska and thus are unlikely to be all seen in the wild at the same time. Clockwise, from top right: parakeet auklets (Gary Schultz), least auklet (Loren Taft/Alaskan Images), breeding rhinoceros auklets, captive birds (Tom Soucek), Cassin's auklet (Lon E. Lauber), crested auklet (Loren Taft/Alaskan Images), and whiskered auklet (Lon E. Lauber).

Throughout the crisis, the little sparrow Scott had rescued as a boy flitted around in the back of his mind. Soon, another special bird entered his life: an American bald eagle whose injured wing Scott was forced to amputate.

One Wing, as Scott called him, clearly

Mergansers are excellent divers and are generalists when it comes to feeding, catching everything from eels (shown) and fish to crustaceans and mollusks. (Harry M. Walker)

could not be returned to the wild. But of more immediate concern to the vet, "we had lots of birds that needed transfusions. I decided that One Wing would be the one we'd use to give blood, to give the others a chance."

Ordinarily, a veterinarian might draw blood from a bird once every two weeks. In the aftermath of the spill, however, Scott sometimes drew blood from One Wing three days in a row. He'd give the bird a day's rest, then draw blood on three more days. Somehow, One Wing survived.

Somehow, One Wing thrived.

"He just got stronger and stronger, and he and I have quite a bond," Scott says. "If we had a mascot, it would be One Wing. He's certainly a bird we rally around."

On a crisp November afternoon, the air is cold in the unheated wooden building where Scott moves down a long corridor. Here and there, he stops to peer into a mew, a small room or holding pen for a bird. Often, he has a few words for the raptor that gazes back: "Hello. Such a fine bird."

Opening a door, Scott steps outside into a long, net-covered flight pen. "Cuk cuk cuk!" he calls to three bald eagles, perched at the far end of the enclosure. The birds regard him closely. Wooden walls rise to meet netting hanging down from overhead. An eagle drops from its perch and flies toward Scott, then swoops up to grasp the netting above. For a moment, the bird hangs from a taloned foot, then it flaps its powerful wings, releases its foot, and flies back to its perch. This one is ready to be released, perhaps at the bald eagle festival in Haines.

Beside the restless flier sits One Wing, and next to him sits his partially blind mate. A decade after One Wing's blood saved his injured fellows, this flight pen is the eagle pair's retirement home.

Leaving the flight pens, Scott relates the story of their construction. In the wake of the oil spill, as some birds regained their health and more arrived in need of care,

Bird TLC ran out of room.

"We needed a place to put birds that were beyond a certain level of healing," Scott says. "We needed a flight pen. There was a colonel in the Army, Col. Wayne Rush, and he said they had some space on Fort Carroll [the Guard base within Fort Richardson] if I wanted to take a look. I did. A falconer, Tim Sell, designed the pens for us. It's a very good design."

Exxon donated money for the project and the public eagerly pitched in. Local businesses offered building supplies, the electrical union donated work.

"In less than three weeks, with volunteer labor, this whole structure was put up," Scott says. "People from every walk of life hammered nails. We had army colonels, attorneys, prostitutes from Fourth Avenue. It was a pretty neat thing because people gave entirely of themselves. They did it just for the birds."

The Science and Sport of Birding

David Sonneborn backs the dusky red-sided Volvo out of his garage and pops open the passenger door. "Let's look for some birds," he says. "Did you bring binoculars?"

He puts the car in gear and begins to slowly wind through the streets around his home, in the Turnagain neighborhood of Anchorage. He scans ahead, to left and right, as he proceeds through familiar surroundings. Approaching a stand of mountain ash, he comments on the appeal

of these ornamental trees for bohemian waxwings, who love their bright red fruit.

"The mountain ash in town used to lose every berry," he says. "The waxwings would eat every one and then disappear. Now, they're staying in town all winter because there are so many mountain ash. And there are more planted every year." The clouds of waxwings often seen swirling along at treetop level around town in fall must be elsewhere just now. We turn toward our first birding stop.

This autumn afternoon, Westchester

Willow ptarmigan run from humans, and if approached too closely, will explode into the air in a flurry of noisy wingbeats. In Denali National Park, these visitors watch from a respectful distance as ptarmigan cross the road. (Harry M. Walker)

Lagoon is thickly dotted with waterfowl. Sonneborn quickly surveys the scene. "Some rare birds have been seen here," he says. Nothing spectacular today. We head toward Anchorage Memorial Park Cemetery,

Arctic shores are the summer home of the Sabine's gull, the only gull occurring in the United States with a forked tail. Photographed on the Colville River Delta on Alaska's North Slope, this one shows summer plumage with its dark gray head. Molting adults have a lighter head. (Gary Schultz)

scanning the trees and sky as we go.

"Have you seen the mockingbird?" Sonneborn asks, as he drives. "No? This thing has been in town for about two years, now. It's a northern mockingbird. We thought it would freeze to death during the winter, but it would sit on top of chimneys and that's how it survived."

The mockingbird is a celebrity among local birders. It frequents the neighborhood west of the cemetery as well as the cemetery itself. Later, as we walk past a house, Sonneborn points. "The mockingbird often sits on that chimney, right there." I look, but the chimney is just a chimney.

Dr. David Sonneborn brings to his avian avocation both the passion of a sportsman and the careful precision of, well, a cardiologist. There is little in his manner that suggests the spiritual bent that Jim Scott brings to his own work with injured birds. But then, spirituality can take many forms.

"Bird-watching has been described as either the most scientific of sports or the most sporting of sciences," Sonneborn says.

Science or sport, whenever he has a free hour, Sonneborn is liable to walk or drive around town, scouting for birds. When he bicycles to work, he takes binoculars. He monitors and contributes to the local Audubon bird hotline, and will go some distance to see anything new or unusual. Recently, when a patient reported seeing a strange bird, Sonneborn drove to Palmer to check it out. "Turned out to be an escaped orange bishop," he says, "a captured bird." Nothing to add to his life list.

Sonneborn started watching birds as a boy, in New York City. He went with his father, who was also a medical doctor, although the elder Sonneborn was not a serious birder.

A half-century later, the younger Sonneborn's life list has grown long and he has a number of record sightings to his credit. "At this point, to see something different, it has to be pretty unusual, but it's a tremendous amount of fun," Sonneborn says. "Look, this is a hobby. I don't know why — it's not rational, and my wife thinks I'm crazy — but ever since I was a kid, it's just been something I enjoy. I like to look at birds."

Approaching the port of Anchorage, Sonneborn points out a bald eagle perched near the top of a tree overlooking Ship Creek. "That eagle sits there all the time, every winter," he says.

Cruising the approach to the public boat ramp south of the port, Sonneborn spots a pair of Barrow's goldeneyes, male and female. Turning back upstream, heading for the old dam site on lower Ship Creek, we pass a series of ponds.

"That one stays open all winter," he says. "There are dippers in there — ever seen one? They walk underwater, they're really neat birds. Short of the gate to Elmendorf Air Force Base gate, Sonneborn turns the Volvo around.

"When I'm birding, I'm looking for little microenvironments," Sonneborn explains, bits of habitat suited to specific birds. It might be a pond with the right kind of bottom for dippers to walk on, a tree with an eagle's-eye vantage point, a stand of mountain ash with berries, a toasty chimney to warm a mockingbird.

Birding with Sonneborn, it quickly becomes apparent that an elite birder is alert and exquisitely attuned to his or her environment, both natural and man-made. A birder sees and stores away countless bits of information for future reference.

Experiencing the world in this way, seeing it, knowing these things, may afford one of the pleasures of birding. An afternoon spent watching birds seems like a good way to counteract stress.

"It is," Sonneborn admits. "But I don't need stress to go birding."

Opening Doors

For a birder blessed with curiosity, bird-watching opens door after door upon the marvelous world around us. One reason birds open doors so effectively is their high visibility. Even in cities, where much of nature is kept at a distance, birds have a real presence. From songbirds in trees, to pigeons and waterfowl that people feed in parks, to peregrine falcons that nest in skyscrapers, birds surround us and make their presence felt.

BELOW LEFT: *Fattening up on grubs for their long trans-Pacific flight to winter in eastern Asia, a northern wheatear young and an adult partake in an age-old ritual of begging and feeding. (Hugh Rose)*

BELOW: Troglodytes troglodytes, *of Greek origin meaning "creeper into holes, a cave dweller," is the only member of the wren family found in Alaska. This winter wren sings a series of high, tinkling warbles and trills that lasts about seven seconds. (Gary Schultz)*

"People have this relationship with birds, it's their connection with nature," George Matz says. "You become familiar with black-capped chickadees, which are pretty common, and all of a sudden you see one that's a little different, more brownish than black," he continues. "Well, that's a boreal chickadee. Then you notice that both birds feed in spruce trees, but the boreal chickadee will be in the higher parts of the tree and the black-capped will be lower. So you learn about their specializations and how they've adapted.

"Next, you go to Girdwood and you find these chestnut-backed chickadees. How come there aren't any chestnut-backed chickadees in Anchorage? Well, chestnut-backed chickadees live in the coastal rainforest, and Girdwood is right on the edge of the coastal rainforest. So you start to see these differentiations that go beyond the birds and into the flora. And the flora depends on rainfall and climate, but it's more than that, it goes into geology. And all of these things are connected, so it deepens not just your appreciation of birds, it deepens your appreciation for life. These threads go in any direction you want."

Wispy down feathers help identify this fox sparrow, sitting on crowberry bushes, as a chick. Down is pushed from the feather follicles of young birds as juvenile feathers grow. (Karen Cornelius)

Jim Scott has witnessed connections of a different sort at his bird rehabilitation clinic. He has seen birds unlock doors not just on the nature around us but on the nature within us, doors into our own human nature.

It turns out that the "Learning" in Bird Treatment and Learning Center is there for a reason. Of course, it makes possible the "TLC" abbreviation, an allusion to the "tender, loving care" lavished on avian patients. And Scott intended the allusion. But birds at the center are not trained, they do not learn in that sense. At the Bird Treatment and Learning Center, it is the humans who learn. The clinic benefits people as well as birds. The healing works both ways.

The deep appeal birds hold for people has roots with many strands. "Everybody wants to fly," Scott begins. "When you're a little kid and you see a bird, you want to fly. That's part of it, but it's not just that. Other parts are the beauty of birds, the amazing variety of colors and shapes, the songs. And the intelligence."

"Being called a bird-brain could really be quite an honor," George Matz agrees. "Birds are more advanced than we are in some respects: in terms of their navigation ability, their spatial recognition. Some of their senses are more acute. Their whole brain is arranged differently than ours."

As fascinating as avian abilities can be — Scott admits he is particularly entranced by the speed and agility of hummingbirds — it is the beauty of birds and their songs to which the veteran veterinarian returns.

"The grumpiest man in the world pays attention when a bird sings a song," Scott says. "I used to take birds that were going to be released, like robins or waxwings, out to some of the old folks homes.

"One time there was a little man, probably in his 80s, in a wheelchair. And he wouldn't say anything, he was just really angry that they had taken him outside. So I walked over and I took a waxwing — I had seven or eight of them to release — and I said, 'Mr. So-and-so, put your hand out.' And he did. And I said, 'I'm going to put this bird in your hand and I want you to put your other hand on top of it. And when you're ready, you can just open the top and your bird will fly away.'

A horned puffin in the Pribilof Islands pulls up grass it will use to line its nest. This alcid family member lays one egg in a short burrow it digs from dirt, usually near a cliff edge, or in a rock crevice it lines minimally with grass and feathers. (Hugh Rose)

"Well, he looked kind of interested. And when he took his hand off the top, the bird didn't fly away, it just kind of sat there and looked around. And it just melted him, it just absolutely melted him. And then it flew away. And I think that's exactly what it was supposed to do. I don't know what they feel or whether they can read our feelings, but that man needed something to put a spark into his day. And then he was just talkative, 'Did you see that? Did you see that? My bird stayed with me a while!' And it was wonderful."

There is another story from the files of the Bird TLC that Scott sometimes tells, another tale of human-avian interactions. But this is a story of more lasting consequence, of deeper transformation.

"We had a woman volunteer whose son was autistic," Scott says. "He was a 10- or 11-year-old boy, and he would be sitting in my waiting room when I came in, because his mom always came early to work on the birds. I'd go by and I'd say hello to him and he'd just look straight ahead, never moved or anything. And he would be there during the two-and-a-half hours that his mom was there working, just sitting there looking in one direction.

"Well, I had some ring-necked doves come in, and they weren't wild birds so it was okay for me to give them away. So I asked her if she felt that he would be interested in the doves. They made soft cooing sounds, they're very pleasant to have around. And she said, 'Well, we could try it.' So I gave him the birds.

"About a month went by, seeing him in the morning all the time and walking by. And I walked by one morning and just as I got by him, I heard this little voice say, 'Thank you, Dr. Scott.'

"I jerked around because he'd never said anything before. But from that point on, when I'd come in in the morning, he would tell me about new things with the birds. Now that boy, he's never going to be a rocket scientist, but he's a grown young man now, he's nearing 20 or so. And he has a job. And he has pride in himself. And he loves his birds. And I want to tell you, that's changing people."

A pair of common ravens, which mate for life, huddle against the Interior's extreme temperature. As one of the state's toughest birds, ravens also seem to thrive in the high Arctic at Prudhoe Bay, where one Christmas Bird Count turned up, after two hours of driving around on icy roads, only "68 hardy ravens." (Hugh Rose)

Compared with our feathered friends of the class Aves, we *Homo sapiens* are newcomers on this Earth. Whether birds evolved during the Jurassic Period, as paleontologists believe, or whether God created creatures of the air on the fifth day, as Genesis would have it, birds soared, sang, migrated, nested, and inhabited the surface of the Earth, nearly from pole to pole, long before human eyes or ears beheld their beauty and grace.

Birds have always pleased and charmed us, always inspired, always instructed those open to their lessons: taught us about themselves, about the natural world we share, the spirit that animates all life, about our inner, human selves.

Go forth, then, and hang a feeder outside your window — and keep it full all winter. Stow binoculars and a bird book in your glove box. Open your eyes, your ears, your mind, your heart.

Raven croaks, chickadee calls. Do you hear?

Past to Present: Alaska's Bird People

By Susan Beeman

Knowledge of Alaska's birds comes from a wealth of different sources spanning more than 250 years. The earliest bits of information were fragmentary observations by generalists whose main task was exploration. Foreign expeditions in the eighteenth and nineteenth centuries brought naturalists along to identify and catalog species, which happened to include birds. After the Alaska Purchase in 1867, and as news of Alaska's natural resources spread, the United States government began sending agents north to set up infrastructure in the territory. In addition to their duties, these men collected bird data from stations around Alaska. More recently, trained ornithologists and bird specialists have devoted years to understanding the state's avian mysteries.

Foreign Exploration Period: 1741-1867

When naturalist Georg Wilhelm Steller set foot on Kayak Island in 1741 (see "Alaska's 'First' Bird" page 44) he initiated a precedent for recording Alaska's natural history. Though Capt. Vitus Bering allowed him few hours on land during their travels to collect data, Steller took note of every creature he encountered. He described swans, cormorants, pigeon guillemots, and other birds of the Shumagin Islands, but is best known in bird circles for the Steller's jay, Steller's sea eagle, the threatened Steller's eider, and the doomed spectacled cormorant, extinct since about

Biologist Paul Flint takes notes on spectacled eider eggs in a nest found on the Yukon-Kuskokwim Delta. Government agencies in Alaska employ many such scientists for bird research. (Roy Corral)

1850. Ninety-nine years after Steller sailed Alaska's waters,

Il'ia G. Voznesenskii, also backed by Russia, collected bird specimens from 1840 to 1849 for the Russian Academy of Sciences. He spent most of his time at Kodiak and Sitka, two of the earliest Russian settlements in Alaska, and made 341 skins of 90 species. Johann Friedrich von Brandt, German director of the Zoological Museum in St. Petersburg in the mid 1800s, and for whom Brandt's cormorant is named, undertook to describe the myriad natural history specimens gathered from Alaska during Russian expeditions. He abandoned the project when the United States bought Alaska in 1867.

English expeditions added further information to sketchy bird data, from Capt. James Cook's meanderings along Alaska's edges in 1778, to Capt. Frederick Beechey's 1826 exploration of the coast between Point Hope and Point Barrow, to the 1850 landing of the *Enterprise* at St. Michael. Aboard was Edward Adams, surgeon and naturalist, who, despite a violent introduction to the region (he discovered and buried the frozen body of shipmate Lt. John J. Barnard one month after Koyukon Natives had murdered him) remained ashore observing the birds of Norton Sound. Adams' detailed notes, however, weren't published until 1878, several years after his death; by then, American scientist William Healy Dall's 1870 book *Alaska and its Resources*, considered the ultimate reference book on Alaska's natural history for many years afterward, had already garnered Dall credit for knowledge of bird life in the area.

American Exploration Period: 1865-1900

Two years before Russia sold Alaska to the United States, the Smithsonian Institution and the Chicago Academy of Sciences funded the Russian-American Telegraph Expedition of 1865, in which Dall participated. Specimens collected during the later-abandoned endeavor were sent to the U.S. National Museum (now the National Museum of Natural History) and the Chicago

Squatting over single eggs, common and thick-billed murres shield their scant nests from a neighboring black-legged kittiwake. These species often nest in mixed colonies. (David Roseneau)

Academy, the latter of which published, in 1869, the first extensive paper on Alaska's birds to appear in English. Spencer Fullerton Baird, the first bird curator at the Smithsonian and originator of the National Museum, named in the report as new Alaska records the yellow wagtail, Aleutian tern, and Cassin's auklet, among others. Baird's sandpiper, common only in northern Alaska, was named after him.

After the Alaska Purchase, the U.S. Army Signal Corps began sending men to the territory to establish meteorological stations. Many of them gathered data on flora and fauna for the Smithsonian in their spare time, the most well-known being Lucien McShan Turner and Edward William Nelson. From 1874 to 1877, Turner, under the direction of Baird, then secretary of the Smithsonian, documented the birds of the St. Michael area until he was replaced by Nelson. Turner, however, had not gotten his fill of Alaska, and after being discharged from the Signal Corps, he re-entered one year later and spent his remaining time in service in the Aleutians. The information he provided included the addition of new Alaska species and subspecies and distribution and habitat of many little-known species. Nelson, stationed at various places throughout western Alaska, including St. Michael, the Yukon-Kuskokwim Delta, and St. Lawrence Island, took a broad view, studying the ecology of these areas and the birds that inhabited them. He later became the third chief of the U.S. Biological Survey, and his publication credits run from the ornithological journal *Auk*, published by the American Ornithologists' Union (AOU), to *National Geographic*. Charles Leslie McKay, also a signal corpsman and stationed at Fort Alexander (now Nushagak) in Bristol Bay in 1881, collected 400 Alaska birds for the National Museum before he

Feeding habits are one key to identifying bird species. In a motion akin to that of a sewing machine needle, short-billed dowitchers jab bill and head up and down in shallow water, foraging for insects on the Kenai Peninsula. (Jon R. Nickles)

drowned in the bay. McKay's bunting is named after him.

Other people reported on Alaska's birds too. U.S. Treasury Agent Henry Wood Elliott, assigned to northern fur seal research, published in 1874 the first comprehensive list of bird colonies in the Pribilof Islands. And included in the famous Harriman Expedition of 1899 were Clinton Hart Merriam, chief of the Biological Survey, George Bird Grinnell, founder of the Audubon Society and editor of *Forest and Stream*, and Robert Ridgeway of the Smithsonian.

1900-1950

Just before the turn of the nineteenth century, Joseph Grinnell, who for more than 30 years headed the Museum of Vertebrate Zoology at the University of California, Berkeley, based himself in Sitka to study local birds. In the spring of 1898, he accompanied a mining party on a hunt for gold. Despite their failure at finding the elusive vein, Grinnell continued his ornithological work as the group moved across northwestern Alaska, fueling his growing interest in bird life. He shared his discoveries on summer birds of Sitka, including petrels and the marbled murrelet,

RIGHT: *Birders and ornithologists looking for golden-crowned sparrows are less likely to spot them in central and northern Alaska than in other regions of the state. A good place to see them is on trails in Chugach State Park. (Tom Walker)*

BELOW RIGHT: *It has long been a custom among bird enthusiasts to name bird species after people. John James Audubon honored his friend Gideon B. Smith, a medical doctor in Baltimore, by naming the Smith's longspur, much less abundant in Alaska than the Lapland longspur. (Hugh Rose)*

on birds of the Kotzebue Sound area, and on nesting habits of the varied thrush. After the 1907 and 1908 Alexander expeditions, financed by Annie M. Alexander, a long-time patron of the museum at Berkeley, Grinnell prepared reports from those two major bird studies in Southeast and Prince William Sound, respectively. In two years, Ms. Alexander and her crew collected more than 1,000 birds and 33 sets of eggs. Harry Schelwald Swarth, a member of the final Alexander expedition (1909), prepared the report for that study in which more than 600 birds were collected. Joseph Scattergood

Dixon also had a hand in making the Alexander expeditions a success. He collected data the first and last years; in 1919 he worked with Swarth in the Stikine River area. His research covered Chicagof, Hinchinbrook, and Admiralty islands; he took notes on the life history and breeding of the semipalmated sandpiper in arctic Alaska; and he even wrote an account of a golden eagle attacking a red fox in the Interior.

Still others continued to contribute to the burgeoning amount of Alaska bird data. H. Boardman Conover published articles and reports in *Auk* and in *Condor*, the journal of the Cooper Ornithological Society, in the early to mid 1900s, including a list of 50 species observed or collected in the Hooper Bay region. Herbert Friedmann published extensively during the first half of the century on topics as diverse as the mourning dove, the Mongolian plover, and avian bones found in archaeological sites. George Willett, employed as a Biological Survey warden on Forrester Island Bird Reservation in Southeast, published numerous papers between 1912 and 1926 that helped later ornithologists piece together bird migration and distribution.

Many naturalists in Alaska around the turn of the twentieth century began to publish their findings in magazines and journals geared toward a wider audience. Another Biological Survey employee, and later director of the Denver Museum of Natural History, Alfred M. Bailey's reports on Alaska's birds appeared in *Condor*, *Natural History*, *Murrelet*, *Outdoor Life*, *Auk*, and *Field and Stream*. He traveled the territory from Southeast to the Bering Sea coast. And any history of fauna in Alaska wouldn't be complete without mention of the Muries. Olaus Johan, his wife Margaret, and his brother Adolph all fed bird facts into the collective body of knowledge during their years of traversing the territory, with Olaus' sketches, paintings, and notes being the most bird-oriented of the three. Olaus arrived in Alaska in 1920 by ship to study caribou, but his interests branched out to include birds too. One spring, he mushed dogs from Nenana, in the Interior, hundreds of miles to Hooper Bay, on the Bering Sea coast, where he gained insight into the nesting habits of ducks, geese, snowy owls, cranes, loons, shorebirds, jaegers, and others. Olaus' research in the Aleutians in 1936 revealed hundreds of birds killed each year by foxes, an introduced species, but it wasn't until 1949 that the first efforts to eradicate foxes from some Aleutian islands were made. Many bird populations never bounced back.

1950-present

The first extensive compilation of information on Alaska's birds came when Ira Noel Gabrielson and Frederick Charles Lincoln published *Birds of Alaska* in 1959, the same year Alaska gained statehood. Gabrielson, who at the time was president of the Wildlife Management Institute, had also served as chief of the Bureau of Biological Survey, now the U.S. Fish and Wildlife Service. He'd traveled extensively throughout Alaska, documenting his avian finds and making 955 skins. Gabrielson and Lincoln, both fellows of the AOU, also drew on published and unpublished documents by all those who'd taken such detailed notes in earlier years. One of those men was Tom J. Cade, a 1950 graduate of the University of Alaska, Fairbanks (UAF), whose publications cover details of such bird behavior as a hawk owl bathing in snow and a rusty blackbird eating mosquitoes while in flight.

More recently, dedicated birders have worked closely with professional ornithologists to expand the wealth of scientific data on Alaska's birds. Malcolm Edward "Pete" Isleib had forged a friendship with Roger Tory Peterson that lead to his love of birds. Isleib came to Alaska with the military in the early 1960s, and lived for many years in Cordova. He made his living as a commercial fisherman, but in the tradition of the pioneering naturalists, he learned about birds in his spare time through reading and talking to ornithologists and birders. He traveled the state in pursuit of avian knowledge and became a self-taught expert on distribution of species. Isleib worked closely with Dr. Brina Kessel, professor of zoology emeritus, dean emeritus, and curator of ornithology emeritus at UAF.

Dr. Kessel's fascination with birds began in childhood. She came to Alaska in the summer of 1951, and took a teaching position at UAF. She was granted full

FACING PAGE: *Whether geared toward hobbyist or serious student, birding tours abound in Alaska. Along the shores of Knight Island in Prince William Sound, visitors are likely to see seabirds, shorebirds, and raptors. (Patrick J. Endres)*

professorship in 1959 and taught for 40 more years. Her species-specific studies related to birds of the taiga and tundra have concentrated in western, central, and northern Alaska; she's been a fellow of the AOU since 1960, holding office as its president from 1992 to 1994; and has published numerous books and professional papers. Many of her books cover specific areas of the state, from the Alaska Peninsula to the Colville River to the upper Tanana Valley. In honor of Dr. Kessel, the University of Alaska now bestows annually the Brina Kessel Medal for Excellence in Science to one of its outstanding science students.

Working closely with Dr. Kessel for several years now, Daniel D. Gibson, ornithology collection manager at the University of Alaska Museum in Fairbanks, has done most of his bird research among the islands that intrigued him as a young boy spinning a globe in Pennsylvania — the Aleutians. His publication credits include books and reports on birds of Adak Island, Katmai National Monument, Shemya Island, and birds in Alaska Native cultures. Some, such as "Bird observations at Ugashik Bay, Alaska Peninsula, 10-17 June 1983," and *Status and distribution of Alaska birds* (1978) were written jointly with Kessel. Gibson was the first ever to lead an exploratory bird tour in the Aleutians and on St. Lawrence Island. Gibson and Kessel are working on a major reference book on birds of Alaska.

Another Fairbanks-based scientist, Leonard J. Peyton, has been catching, banding, and releasing redpolls from his back-yard for 32 years. He considers it a hobby, but it's one that takes up much of his time. He's also done extensive studies on bird sounds. From 1967 to 1985, he traveled Alaska recording bird songs and calls, many of which are featured on the 1999 *Bird Songs of Alaska* CD produced by the Cornell Laboratory of Ornithology.

The husband and wife team of Colleen Handel and Bob Gill, both research wildlife biologists with the Alaska Biological Science Center, have studied the state's bird populations for 25 years. Gill is project leader for shorebird research in the state, and has been instrumental in shorebird conservation planning at national and international levels.

Theodore G. "Thede" Tobish, like Gibson, grew up in Pennsylvania. He came to Alaska in 1973, and has been active with the Anchorage chapter of the National Audubon Society, leading the group as its president from 1980 to 1984. Tobish is the Alaska regional editor for the journal *North American Birds*.

Also active in Alaska's birding community is R.L. "Buzz" Scher, a geotechnical engineer by day, an avid birder by all other hours of day and night. When he was 10 years old, his father started taking him bird-watching, and his Boy Scout troop offered bird study as part of its life sciences curriculum. When Scher was 12, he rode the ferry from Maine to Nova Scotia by himself, and while standing out in the breeze on the bow of the boat,

Leonard J. Peyton displays a bird trap he uses to catch redpolls in his backyard in Fairbanks. Over the years, he has banded and released more than 20,000, hoping to discover more about their migration patterns. (Roy Corral)

he struck up a conversation with a man who advised him, "If you really like birding, don't become an ornithologist. Keep it as your hobby." What began as a hobby turned, over time, into an obsession, Scher's own term for it. In 1979, he moved to Alaska and has been to the Aleutians, Southeast, Barrow — all over the state in

search of birds. He is the author and publisher of *Field Guide to Birding in Anchorage* (1989).

Countless others have brought their brief sightings and hard-won observations to the treasury of Alaska bird facts, attesting to the resolve of those who study birds. Often camouflaged by their

surroundings, and usually wary of people, birds are not the easiest animal to study. Long hours and patience are characteristic of both professional ornithologists and passionate birders, and their dedication has filled a multitude of gaps in the web of bird knowledge. Still, there are mysteries yet to be discovered. •

EDITOR'S NOTE: *Scientist and economist George Matz is the author of several articles on ecology and on the economic value of the environment. In addition, he wrote* World Heritage Wilderness, *Vol. 26, No. 2, of* ALASKA GEOGRAPHIC®. *For the past several years he has been president of the Anchorage chapter of the National Audubon Society.*

What Bird Is That?

By George Matz

My friend Scott Foster is the ultimate "lumper." In birding jargon a lumper is someone who prefers to lump together bird identification characteristics so there are fewer subspecies, or even species. Birding is simpler with lumping. In contrast are the splitters, who contend that even the slightest differences are enough to split a species into a separate subspecies or even into a new species. Splitting creates more challenges for birders astute enough to discern obscure variations in bird plumage and other identifying characteristics.

When I lived in Juneau in the 1980s, Scott and I kayaked the fjords, bays, and

FACING PAGE: With talons as sharp as knives, an osprey grips its next meal. As it flies away with its catch, the osprey will turn the fish so its head points forward, reducing wind drag on the load. The bird usually returns to the same tree nearby to feast. (Tom J. Ulrich)

straits of Southeast. We routinely saw a variety of birds and I would usually try to identify each species. Scott was often amused at my attempts to get a better look at some duck bobbing on the water or a songbird flitting through the top of a spruce. He would jest, "Why don't you use my system? It's easier and you'll never be wrong." Scott would then demonstrate: "That bird is a water bird," or "That bird is obviously a tree bird." He didn't even need binoculars or a field guide.

While I have to agree that Scott's system was simpler, I still wanted to know what species I was observing. Being able to identify the species of bird is not only the essence of birding, but the first step in learning more about birds, their behavior, and their environments. Once you become familiar with a bird, you will discover intriguing differences between species and

reasons for these differences. And knowing which species are typical for an area opens a gate to understanding more about the surrounding environment. Some species have specific habitat requirements and their presence indicates the type of ecosystem nearby. The Townsend's warbler, for instance, breeds in mature coniferous forests of Alaska and the Pacific Northwest. The Townsend's is an indicator species for this type of habitat. Conversely, some species are habitat generalists. The raven survives year-round in almost any kind of habitat in northern and western North America from the cold of the North Slope in winter to the scorching heat of Southwest deserts.

Bird identification has the advantage of being as simple or as complex as you want it to be. Based on my experience teaching a beginners' birding class at Anchorage Community Schools, I know there are a

A change in plumage signals the changing season for willow ptarmigan. While they peck at dead willow leaves, these birds' feathers are switching from the mottled brown of summer to all white for winter camouflage. (Hugh Rose)

216 are out of their normal range and do not breed in Alaska. That leaves about 264 species that either reside here or migrate here to breed, less than three percent of the world's total.

The number of species can be narrowed even further by considering just those that are likely to be seen in a certain ecoregion. According to Robert Armstrong's *Guide to the Birds of Alaska* (1995), the biologically rich temperate rainforest of Southeast has about 170 species of birds that are common or uncommon at any season. The transitional climate and forest of the Southcoastal region has 157 species that are either common or uncommon. The boreal forest of the Interior, including the central part of the Kenai Peninsula, has 128 species. The mountains and coastal plain of the Arctic Slope have just 71 species of common or uncommon birds. Notice that the number of species decreases as the latitude and severity of the climate increases.

Some of the birds that are common or uncommon in the coastal areas of western Alaska are rare or accidental in the rest of the state. For instance, the Southwestern region (Bristol Bay, Alaska Peninsula, and

lot of people who want to become more familiar with their neighborhood birds and species they might see camping, hiking, or boating. In Alaska this means 20 to 40 species for sure, and maybe another 10 or 20 by lumping together species that have less certain identification, e.g. chickadee instead of black-capped, boreal, or chestnut-backed chickadee. It's easy to know that a bird is a chickadee, but not always easy to know what species.

Unless you are instantly familiar with a species, bird identification begins by narrowing the possibilities. To present the big picture first, there are nearly 10,000 species of birds in the world. Slightly more than 2,000 occur in North America (from the Panama Canal north), of which more than 700 breed in the United States and Canada. According to the *Checklist of Alaska Birds* compiled by Daniel D. Gibson of the University of Alaska Museum, the state has 445 documented species and about 35 unsubstantiated ones. Of these 480 species,

the Aleutians) has 151 species that are common or uncommon, including the black-footed albatross, red-legged kittiwake, and least auklet. The Western region (coastal tundra from Bristol Bay to the Seward Peninsula) has 134 bird species that are either common or uncommon, including the bristle-thighed curlew and yellow wagtail.

Season also makes a big difference in the number of species you are likely to see. In winter, Alaska birding is limited. Most species migrate somewhere. Ptarmigan remain in the area but move lower on the mountainsides. Loons and diving ducks leave their inland nesting areas to winter in the Gulf of Alaska where seawater remains open. Most songbirds leave the state altogether. Juneau typically records 80 to 90 species during its Christmas Bird Count, Anchorage 40 to 50; Fairbanks usually comes up with 20 to 30 species.

Feeders provide some of the best birding opportunities. According to Project FeederWatch, the most frequently reported resident species at feeders in Alaska, the Yukon, and the Northwest Territories are black-capped and boreal chickadees, downy and hairy woodpeckers, pine siskins, red-

Migrating surf scoters mill around while resting in the waters of Lynn Canal, in Southeast, on their way north to nest. (Hugh Rose)

breasted nuthatches, common redpolls, pine grosbeaks, black-billed magpies, and common ravens.

Regardless of your level of birding expertise, you will want to have at least one of the many field guides that are now available, some covering all of North America and others covering specific regions or states. Most field guides include a map for each species illustrating its breeding range and winter range, or year-round range. These maps can quickly tell you

whether the species you thought you saw is at all likely. If you're in Alaska and see a bird that reminds you of a blue jay, a quick check of the range map will show that it's not. The bird is probably a Steller's jay, which has a crest like the blue jay and is common in spruce/hemlock forests.

In addition, you'll want a checklist covering the area you are birding. Checklists usually include all the species that have been documented within a certain area. Most checklists indicate the seasons that a species

Steller's jays, named after eighteenth-century naturalist Georg W. Steller, inhabit coastal forests along Alaska's southern edge. With a conspicuous crest and blue wings and tail, they are rarely mistaken for any other bird. (Roy Corral)

Alaska's "First" Bird

A flash of iridescent cobalt blue streaks through spruce and birch trees in an Anchorage neighborhood. The sharp *shack!-shack!-shack!* of a Steller's jay bounces between houses, and the crested bird lands briefly on a bough before flying off in its characteristic flap and glide pattern.

The Steller's jay was named after Georg Wilhelm Steller, a German naturalist aboard the *St. Peter* captained by explorer Vitus Bering in 1741. On July 31, with little time to collect specimens, Steller sent his hunter, Thomas Lepikhin, to shoot a few birds for examination while the crew explored the coast of Kayak Island near the Copper River Delta. The bright blue, crested bird Lepikhin brought back attracted Steller's curiosity. He recognized it as a cousin of the American blue jay, and knew that they'd reached America. The Steller's jay holds the spotlight as Alaska's first scientifically described bird.

Today, we know *Cyanocitta stelleri* as a member of the Corvidae family, exhibiting habits similar to those of other jays. The Steller's jay is adaptable, has a thick bill used to hammer and pry, but also thin enough to probe, and its bold nature makes it a joy to watch. Its screams mimicking the red-tailed hawk are surprisingly accurate.

During courtship, the male Steller's jay feeds the female and jumps around her, often changing direction in midair. The pair nests at least 10 feet off the ground in conifers, its nest formed of twigs and held together with mud. The female lays three to four pale green, lightly spotted eggs, and both parents defend the nest. The plumage of immature Steller's jays is duller and more grayish compared to that of adults.

This species eats a varied diet of seeds, berries, eggs, and chicks of small birds; it also pecks at carcasses. Cracks in trees and branches serve as hiding places for food bits stored for later use. It lives in coniferous or mixed coniferous-deciduous forests, and has short wings compared to its 11 1/2-inch body length. A long, rounded tail acts as a rudder to help it steer through dense forests. Steller's jays are common year-round in Southeast and along Southcentral's coasts. In recent years they seem to be expanding their range into upper Cook Inlet. •

can be expected and its relative abundance. Several terms indicate abundance, from common to rare, with casual, accidental, and vagrant being used to describe species that have been observed in the area but are outside their usual range.

Both field guides and checklists are organized by family groups, beginning with the most primitive family from an evolutionary perspective. The Gaviidae family, or loons, will be the first family listed, followed by several families of seabirds and waterfowl. In Alaska, there are 37 families of birds (not counting accidentals) that can be seen on land and inland waters and three pelagic (living in open seas) families (albatrosses, shearwaters, and petrels) that are usually seen from boats far offshore.

Some of these families are large and complex, like the Anatidae that includes ducks, geese, and swans. Others include just one or two species; the Cinclidae has only one species in North America, the American dipper. Each family is divided into one or more genera. The two-part scientific name for a bird begins with its genus, which is capitalized, followed by the species, which is not capitalized. If there are subspecies or races, the scientific name will have a third part. For example, the Arctic subspecies of the dunlin that breeds on the North Slope is called *Calidris alpina arcticola*.

Of course, common names do not follow this systematic classification. In the past, the name of a well-known ornithologist was sometimes bestowed on a species, serving as its common name. Now, common names usually refer to some identifying characteristic. A good example is Audubon's warbler, which the American Ornithologists' Union lumped with the myrtle warbler in 1972, renaming it the yellow-rumped warbler, a songbird common throughout most of Alaska that has a bright yellow patch of feathers above the base of its tail.

Species of birds within the same family tend to have many of the same characteristics. Having some knowledge about which bird families might be found in your area and their general features can help when you are trying to identify an unknown bird. Knowing the family directs you to the appropriate section of a field guide. To

Predominantly red, male pine grosbeaks are some of Alaska's most colorful birds. Females, however, are gray with a tinge of yellow on their head and rump. Despite their name, pine grosbeaks are classified as finches rather than being in the grosbeak family. (Tom Walker)

LEFT: *Nearly the same size and shape as a sandhill crane, the great blue heron can be distinguished in flight from a crane by the way it holds its neck doubled back, with its head against its shoulders. Cranes fly with their neck stretched straight out. This great blue heron stands on a rock along the shore of Tongass Narrows near Ketchikan. (Hall Anderson)*

BELOW: *Olive-sided flycatchers typically lay three eggs in a nest formed of grass, moss, lichen, and other bits of organic debris, building it near the end of a horizontal conifer limb. Black spruce, like this one, tends to grow crooked in muskegs, and makes an ideal home for these members of the tyrant flycatchers. (James L. Davis)*

FACING PAGE: *Loon chicks, covered at first only in down, can get waterlogged and drown. The solution is to climb onto their parents' back for a ride. After 10 days to two weeks, chicks learn to swim and dive on their own. (Arne Grisham)*

Origins

By George Matz

Which came first, the chicken or the egg? From the perspective of evolution, the creation of a new species of bird may occur when there is a change in the gene pool of a population of interbreeding birds. The genetic change that created the chicken must have been evident first in the egg. Once the egg hatched, there was a chicken.

When Charles Darwin visited the Galapagos Islands in the Pacific Ocean west of Ecuador in 1831, he noticed each of the species of finches on the islands had different-shaped beaks and that the shape of the beak enabled different feeding habits. This observation contributed to the development of Darwin's theory of evolution, which states that variation within a species enables an organism to better adapt to its environment and improve its ability to survive.

Darwin presented his controversial theory in *The Origin of Species* (1859). Two years later, a fossil dating from the Jurassic period (208-145 million years ago) was found in a limestone quarry in Bavaria, Germany that had features of both bird and reptile, adding evidence but also fuel to the fire ignited by Darwin's theory.

The Archaeopteryx fossil had wings and primary feathers but a reptilian jaw with numerous teeth. It evolved from an ancient line of dinosaur-type reptiles known as thecodonts that were bipedal, like all modern birds. Although this was a primitive bird, it was a dead end in bird evolution and is not directly related to modern birds.

Still, modern birds and reptiles have much in common. The scales on birds' legs and some beaks are identical to reptile scales. Birds and

reptiles lay eggs and their young develop an egg tooth that is used in hatching. They have a similar arrangement of internal organs and some skeletal traits. But to enable flying, birds evolved feathers, bodies with light beaks instead of heavy teeth and jaws, wings rather than front legs, and extensions to the lungs called air sacs that penetrate certain bones and parts of the body cavity. Birds share fewer similarities with mammals: Both are warm-blooded and have a four-chambered heart with double circulation. Unlike other classes of animals, birds and mammals care for their offspring.

But it seems that nature always adds exceptions to the rule. For instance, some reptiles have air sacs (sea turtles) and care for their

young (crocodiles). There are some flightless birds (penguins), some mammals lay eggs (duck-billed platypuses), and others fly (bats).

The evolution of birds from reptiles occurred because of natural selection that was driven by the adaptation of animals to their environment. These adaptations gave an animal a competitive advantage within its existing environment or the ability to exploit a new environment. While these mechanisms are as old as life itself, they are as current as a newborn. Adaptation continues to create morphological, physiological, and behavioral changes in birds and other animals, enabling them to survive in an ever-changing world. •

FAR LEFT: *Signs of life emerge slowly from a mew gull egg as the chick pecks its way out of the protective shell. Most bird embryos develop an egg tooth atop their bill, a hard knob that helps them "hammer" their way into the world. (Tom Walker)*

LEFT: *Loons, such as the yellow-billed loon shown here, are considered the most primitive of all bird families. Designed for swimming, loons' legs are positioned far back on their body. They can take only a few awkward steps at a time on land. (Tom Walker)*

illustrate, if it looks like a hummingbird, it probably is. Turning to that part of a field guide, the maps show that the only hummingbird typically found in Southeast and the Prince William Sound area is the rufous hummingbird. As you become more skilled, you will recognize similarities between species that belong to other less distinct families, such as thrushes and warblers.

Field Marks

Identifying a species of bird is often based on its field marks. A prerequisite for using field marks is having some familiarity with bird morphology, or the form and structure of birds. Most species have something distinctive about their plumage, shape, or size that sets them apart from other species within the same family or genus. An example is the red-breasted nuthatch, a year-round resident of Southeast and Southcentral. Knowing where the breast is, you know where to look for this field mark. However, if the field guide says that the color of the primary feathers on the glaucous-winged gull is the same as on the rest of the wing or that the mallard has a blue speculum, that part of the body may not be so obvious. Consequently, the introduction for most field guides has an illustration that labels typical bird body parts and feathers. Turning to this illustration, you can quickly see that the primary feathers are the long feathers located at the end of the wing and the speculum is an iridescent

patch of feathers that many birds have near the middle of their wing.

Plumage provides key field marks. Some birds, like the male harlequin duck, are so brightly plumaged that it would be difficult to confuse them with any other species. However, the female harlequin, as with most ducks, is a drab brown, and can be hard to identify if she is not beside the male. With some songbirds, the female is so different that she actually looks like another species. A good example is the pine grosbeak, a relatively common resident of coniferous forests throughout Alaska. The male has a reddish-pink body, while the female is gray with a yellowish tinge to the upper body.

Some species, like the black-billed magpie that is common in the state south of the Alaska Range, has the same plumage all year, whether as juveniles or adults. Other species molt, or change their plumage, with the seasons. The breeding plumage for many

TOP LEFT: *The most common shorebird in Glacier Bay in the fall is the red-necked phalarope, a sandpiper whose toes are edged with a scalloped membrane, giving them the ability to swim like a duck. The female phalarope, shown here, is more brightly colored than the male, and studies have shown that females' testosterone level is sometimes higher than males', a probable explanation for why females court males and male phalaropes stay on the nest to brood and raise the chicks. (Don Cornelius)*

ABOVE: *Singing from its perch in a dead spruce tree, a white-crowned sparrow utters a plaintive, wheezy, six-note song. The syrinx, an organ unique to birds, is located at the lower end of the windpipe and acts as a vibration chamber through which air is expelled. Special muscles regulate how much pressure is applied to change pitch, in much the same way a violin is played. (James L. Davis)*

Bohemian waxwings frequent ornamental mountain ash trees throughout Anchorage, swooping as a flock from tree to tree and often perching on rooftops or tall cottonwoods to rest. (Roy Corral)

ducks, shorebirds, and songbirds is brighter and more distinctive than their winter plumage. The drab winter plumage reduces the differences between species, making identification more difficult. Fortunately for us in Alaska, we see all of our species when they are in their breeding plumage and at their brightest.

In addition to seasonal variations, some species have different juvenile plumages. In some cases, juvenile plumage lasts just a year; with bald eagles and gulls it may last three or four years and change year to year. Gulls make identification even harder by hybridizing. Glaucous-winged and herring gulls often interbreed, resulting in a bird that has features of each species. Identifying juvenile and hybrid gulls can be frustrating for even the most experienced birder. Beginners are advised to take the lumper approach here.

A plumage variation that occurs with some species is color. Birds of the same species that have different-colored plumage are called morphs. A good example among Alaska birds is the Harlan's hawk, formerly considered a distinct species but now classi-fied a subspecies of the red-tailed hawk. The widespread red-tailed hawk has several subspecies, each having either a dark or rufous color variation. The overall plumage for the Harlan's subspecies is much darker than the typical red-tailed hawk.

Size can figure prominently in identifi-cation, particularly with several very similar species. Downy and hairy woodpeckers, two species fairly common throughout Alaska's forests, look nearly identical except for over-all body size and length of bill. The hairy's body is about 50 percent larger than that of the downy and its bill is about twice as long. The Northwestern crow, common in coastal forests, is distinguished from its cousin, the common raven, by its smaller body and bill.

A bird's shape can be a distinguishing feature, particularly in poor light when the only thing you can see is a silhouette. If, in the darkening twilight, you see the silhouette of a fairly large bird perched in the top of a tree with two tufts sticking out from its head, you can be certain that it is a great horned owl. The shape of a great blue heron, the only wading bird that breeds in Alaska, has a long neck and legs that can't be confused with any other bird here. Although many songbirds have similar shapes, the long tail of the black-billed magpie is distinguishing.

Flight pattern also helps identification. If I see a bird zipping through the forest with an undulating flight, I know it's a woodpecker, even if there isn't time for a good look. The brown creeper, among the smallest forest birds in Southeast and Southcentral year-round, blends well with the trees it clings to. But its distinctive flight pattern gives it away. The creeper lands near the bottom of a tree, then spirals up the trunk as it looks for spiders and other food. About half way up, it will take flight again, and land near the base of the next tree, creating a "z" pattern.

Raptors (the eagle and hawk family and the falcon family) not only have different flight patterns among species, but also distinctive body shapes. Combining flight pattern with the shape of a raptor's wings and tail provides another identification clue. The length and width of their wings and the length and shape of their tail indicate whether a particular species soars or flies with powerful wingbeats. Red-tailed and rough-legged hawks, two species of the buteo genus that are fairly common in most of Alaska during the summer, have wide wings and tails just right for catching thermal uplifts, enabling them to soar with

little effort while searching for mice and other prey. The accipiter genus of hawks, which includes the northern goshawk, has a long tail, short wings, and flies with several quick wing beats and a glide. This pattern enables accipiters to easily maneuver between trees as they chase smaller birds. The falcon family, including the peregrine, among the fastest of birds, has long, powerful wings that bend back at the wrist, allowing these birds to dive on their prey at high speeds.

With shorebirds, size, shape, and color of bill and legs often identify the species. A good example is the yellowlegs. Obviously the two species, greater and lesser, have yellow legs. In addition to being slightly

Largely an Alaska and Russian species, the threatened spectacled eider nests along the Bering Sea and Arctic Ocean coasts from the mouth of the Kuskokwim River north to the Colville River Delta. It favors brackish pools for feeding and consumes a variety of invertebrates, plants, and berries. (John W. Warden)

smaller, the lesser yellowlegs' bill is about as long as the length of its head. The greater yellowlegs has a bill that is noticeably longer than the length of its head.

Male hooded mergansers (captive bird shown) can raise and lower their black-bordered crest. When the crest is down, the white head patch appears as a streak. In Alaska, this species is most likely to be found in river valley woodlands in Southeast. (Tom Soucek)

Bird Calls and Songs

Each species of bird has distinct combinations of calls and songs that aid identification. Calls are short notes that serve as warnings, location beacons between parents and young, and other necessities. Songs are more melodious and are usually sung by males to attract females and to defend their territory. With Empidonax (genus) flycatchers, the song is the most reliable way to identify the species. The alder flycatcher, which breeds in Southeast, Southcentral, and the Interior, looks like the Hammond's flycatcher, which breeds mostly in the Interior, and the Pacific-slope flycatcher of Southeast. The slight difference in their shade of olive-green is indistinguishable when the bird is half hidden by leaves that are about the same size and color as the bird. But their songs are distinctly different. The alder flycatcher has a harsh two-syllable call that sounds like "free beer," which should be easy to remember on a warm summer day. Both the Hammond and Pacific-slope flycatchers have songs that are better heard on a tape or CD than described. Incidentally, if you have an older field guide you might not find the Pacific-slope flycatcher. It used to be called the western flycatcher, but this species was recently split into two, the Pacific-slope and Cordilleran flycatchers. Like they say, you need a score card to tell the players, or in the case of birds, you need a recent field guide.

Not only does every species have its own call and song, there are often dialects within a species. If you listen to the call of a fox sparrow on a birding tape, it may sound much different than the fox sparrow you just heard. That is because there are about 18 subspecies of fox sparrows and many more dialects. Even the fox sparrows that live on the upper Hillside area of Anchorage have a slightly different dialect than those that live on the lower Hillside. Nevertheless, a bird's song is not only a

RIGHT: *Mountain bluebirds are rare in Alaska but have been documented in nearly all regions of the state. Females are brownish overall with a wash of blue of their wings and tail, while males are bright blue. (Tom Soucek)*

FAR RIGHT: Lanius excubitor, *Latin for "watchful butcher," describes the northern shrike's habit of impaling prey on thorns or broken twigs and hanging it from the crotch of a tree. Here, a 10-inch northern shrike perches on a willow branch on Alaska's North Slope. (Gary Schultz)*

reliable way to locate it, but one of the best ways to confirm what species you just saw.

Experienced birders identify more birds by their call or song than by their field marks. Some, such as the tiny ruby-crowned kinglet that likes to yodel from the top of a tall spruce, would be nearly impossible to identify if it weren't for its repetitive notes that are fairly easy to remember once heard. But you can be tricked. Some birds mimic their neighbors. I was once on a field trip at Creamer's Field in Fairbanks when our group clearly observed both an orange-crowned warbler and a dark-eyed junco singing on the same shrub. These birds have slightly different songs, but what was confusing in this case was that the junco sounded more like the warbler and vice versa. If we hadn't clearly seen each bird, we would have misidentified both.

Another important tool is a tape or CD of bird songs. Avid birders spend at least a couple of hours every spring listening to bird song tapes or CDs to refamiliarize themselves with the species they are likely to hear when spring migration gets under-way. A CD by the Cornell Laboratory of Ornithology entitled *Bird Songs of Alaska* (see page 96) includes 260 species that occur in the state. Most of these recordings were made in Alaska, minimizing the dialect problem.

Other Characteristics

A bird's behavior can add another important clue to solving an identification puzzle. While some aspects of bird behavior may take a trained eye to detect, there are traits that are just plain obvious. For instance, phalaropes have a distinctive way of feeding. Each of the three species in this

A horny tube atop this storm-petrel's beak allows the bird to expel excess salt it ingests during eating and drinking on the open sea. Alaska waters host two species from this family, the Leach's storm-petrel (shown here) and the fork-tailed storm-petrel. (Lon. E. Lauber)

genus (the most common in Alaska being the red-necked) twirl in shallow water like wind-up toys. This furious action stirs up larvae and other food buried in the mud on the bottom of a pond, making easy pickings for the phalarope. Another example of distinctive behavior is the up and down bobbing of the spotted sandpiper as it stands on the bank of a stream. This behavior is noticeable from a distance and is often easier to discern than its spotted breast.

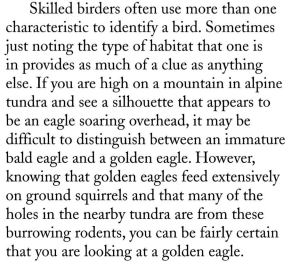

Skilled birders often use more than one characteristic to identify a bird. Sometimes just noting the type of habitat that one is in provides as much of a clue as anything else. If you are high on a mountain in alpine tundra and see a silhouette that appears to be an eagle soaring overhead, it may be difficult to distinguish between an immature bald eagle and a golden eagle. However, knowing that golden eagles feed extensively on ground squirrels and that many of the holes in the nearby tundra are from these burrowing rodents, you can be fairly certain that you are looking at a golden eagle.

Four species of swallows are common throughout most of Alaska (tree, violet-green, bank, and cliff); Southeast also has the barn swallow. Although all swallows have a distinctive flight pattern, their rapid sweeps and turns make it difficult to determine which species you are observing. Nesting habitat can provide a good clue. Tree and violet-green swallows are cavity nesters, nesting in holes of trees. They also like bird houses, providing the houses are not too close to each other. On the other hand, bank and cliff swallows nest in colonies. A group of holes in a steep riverbank, such as along the Chulitna, or a highway cut will likely contain bank swallow nests. Cliff swallows build a cluster of adobe-style nests made of mud stuck to a crevasse in a cliff or the undersides of a building. Mud banks of rivers flowing into the lower end of Lake Clark offer

Bald Eagle: National Bird, State Icon

An estimated 50,000 bald eagles, more than in all of the contiguous United States combined, live in Alaska year-round. Chosen in 1782 as a national symbol of freedom and strength, the species was nonetheless considered "vermin" long after killing them became illegal. Alaska's territorial government paid a bounty for bald eagles until the federal government extended its Bald Eagle Protection Act to cover the newly formed state of Alaska in 1959.

Bald eagles now thrive here, with the largest populations occurring in southern coastal areas from Southeast to Prince William Sound to the Aleutian Islands. Residents of communities in these areas often see eagles daily, sitting on branches, soaring high overhead, or, contrary to the bird's noble image, scavenging food scraps from the local dump.

Artistic representations of the bald eagle abound in Alaska's towns and within Alaska Native artwork. In downtown Ketchikan, a carved wooden eagle stands many feet taller than its Tlingit sculptor, Nathan Jackson. A bronze Alaska statehood monument in Anchorage combines a bust of President Dwight Eisenhower, the Alaska flag, and a bald eagle. An eagle in flight graces Alaska State Park signs.

Attesting, too, to the eagle's prominence are all the lakes, rivers, creeks, bays, and islands named in the bird's honor — even a town on the banks of the Yukon River called — what else? — Eagle. •

good habitat. Barn swallows are attracted to the same kind of conditions that cliff swallows like, but tend to be in smaller groups.

Identifying birds requires eyes, ears, and being able to quickly recognize some pattern of identification. Sometimes the quick look reveals just a glimpse of a field mark or part of a distinctive flight pattern. Birds seldom seem to offer a field guide

A bald eagle's eyesight is at least three times sharper than a human's, lending credibility to the term "eagle eyes." Its sense of smell is thought to be relatively poor, while its hearing is about the same as a human's. (Alissa Crandall)

view before flying off. That is why it pays to become familiar with several aspects of a bird's identity.

ABOVE: *A colony of double-crested cormorants nests at Lake Louise, a popular recreation area. Tall nests built of sticks elevate the birds, giving them a better command of their territory. (Don Cornelius)*

ABOVE RIGHT: *Weighing only one-half of an ounce, a savannah sparrow barely bends the tip of a lupine stalk along Turnagain Arm, southeast of Anchorage. These birds are common throughout much of Alaska, and are most often found in open grassy meadows. (Gary Schultz)*

Identification of Some Common Species

Following are brief descriptions of birds that should be fairly easy to identify and are common throughout most of Alaska. Several bird families are represented.

PACIFIC LOON:

There are five species of loons in the world and each breeds in Alaska. The Pacific loon, which breeds throughout the state except for Southeast, has a typical loon shape while floating on the water, but is slightly smaller than the common loon. Breeding Pacific loons have a smooth gray head and a black patch on their neck with white stripes. Its series of calls are similar to the common loon, but higher pitched and not as smooth.

RED-NECKED GREBE:

Grebes have loonlike shapes and a similar diving style, but they are smaller. The red-necked grebe breeds throughout Alaska except on the North Slope. When floating in a shallow lake or pond, its reddish-brown neck and large white patch on its lower face are easy to distinguish. This bird builds a floating nest among weeds, making it quite visible most of the time. When loons and grebes nest on the same pond, adult loons sometimes attack and kill grebe chicks.

DOUBLE-CRESTED CORMORANT:

Cormorants are dark birds with noticeably long bills, necks, and bodies, ideal for diving and catching fish. They nest mostly in rocky, coastal areas, although a colony of double-crested cormorants nests on an island in Lake Louise near Glennallen. The double-crested cormorant has a yellow-orange pouch near its bill and breeding adults have a tuft of feathers on either side of their head, hence the name double-crested. Cormorants are often seen flying in harbor areas and the double-crested can be identified by the kink in its outstretched neck.

AMERICAN WIGEON:

The American wigeon is a small puddle duck and one of Alaska's most common waterfowl. Like all ducks, the male and female are quite different. The male has a

Immature sandhill cranes can be distinguished from older birds by their lack of a red skin patch on their forehead. Cranes stand nearly three feet tall and have a wingspan of almost seven feet. (Tom Culkin)

green streak running along the side of its head, similar to the green-winged teal. However, the white stripe along the top of its head is distinctive, even when mixed in with other ducks. Females have a nondescript grayish-brown head and reddish-brown body. Up close, both have a bluish bill with a black tip.

SPRUCE GROUSE:

Grouse and ptarmigan were like chickens to Alaska's early pioneers, their plump bodies and breasts providing a good meal. Spruce, blue, and ruffed grouse are similar but have different ranges. The most noticeable difference in appearance is in the tail, particularly when fanned out. Spruce grouse inhabit the boreal forest. They have a black tail with a reddish-brown band at the end. Males have red eye combs. When breeding, males puff out their feathers and spread their tails in a display of dominance.

SANDHILL CRANE:

Cranes are not only among the tallest birds in the world, but the oldest. Their haunting call echoes a primeval connection.

Snowy Owls of the Arctic

By Rodney Griffiths

EDITOR'S NOTE: *Rodney Griffiths is a freelance nature photographer who lives in Oxford, England and travels the globe in search of compelling images of birds and other animals. In addition to being published in previous issues of* ALASKA GEOGRAPHIC®, *his work has appeared in* Birdwatch, Birdwatching, Freelance Photographer, *and others. The Discovery Channel's program* Wild About Animals *has featured Griffiths' bald eagle photos.*

In the Arctic, where the summer sun never sets, the snowy owl hunts by necessity in daylight. Although at times it glides silently over barren tundra in search of rodents, its technique for catching its most preferred prey, lemmings, is to sit motionless, sometimes for hours, on the summit of a hummock. From there, its keen eyes can detect the slightest movement.

Owls in general use a combination of sight and hearing to detect prey, but tundra, the prime habitat of snowy owls, is soft and quiet, muffling the sounds of small rodents. Consequently, snowy owls have comparatively small auditory canals and poor hearing. In years when lemmings and voles are scarce, snowy owls eat hares, fish, and other birds.

Snowy owls reside along the North Slope and western coastal areas of Alaska as far south as Bristol Bay. The low plains of Point Barrow are a favorite nesting site; Barrow and Nome offer the best chances of a summer sighting. The owls breed on tundra on the mainland, on some of the Aleutian Islands, and on the Pribilof Islands, scratching a shallow nest from a dry hummock and typically laying five to seven white eggs. In years of abundant prey, clutches of 16 eggs have been reported, but when the lemming population is low, snowy owls may not nest at all.

Spasmodically and unpredictably in some winters, large numbers of snowy owls migrate southward and spend a few weeks in the lower states of Canada or the upper states of the contiguous United States. Attempts to correlate this movement with a drop in lemming numbers have not proved conclusive. During these winter irruptions southward, many birds arrive near starvation. They can be spotted sitting on power poles, hayricks, and barn roofs and are easily approached. By late January, however, most have returned north to more familiar territory.

Back in Alaska, the snowy owl is a wary bird, taking flight when any human comes within several hundred yards — not surprising, since Eskimos have long hunted it for food. This largest of arctic predatory birds remains silent during winter, but on its breeding grounds in summer emits loud croaks and harsh whistles. •

LEFT: *Male snowy owls actively defend their mate, nest, and chicks from intruders, often employing the "injured bird act" to lure predators away. They have also been known to fly at and attack humans who approach too closely. (Rodney Griffiths)*

FACING PAGE: *Posts, rooftops, and power poles make good vantage points for snowy owls near human civilization. (Rodney Griffiths)*

band below that. The band extends across a white breast. Other plovers that do not visit Alaska also have this band, but the semipalmated differs in also having a dark brown back. Plovers are noted for performing a wounded wing act to distract intruders approaching its nest.

WESTERN SANDPIPER:

The western sandpiper descends on Alaska's coastal beaches in flocks of thousands when they return in early May on their way to breeding grounds in western and northern Alaska. This species is one of the peeps, a group of small sandpipers that look fairly similar. What distinguishes a breeding-plumaged western from a semi-palmated sandpiper, even at some distance, is its rufous-colored shoulders and head.

COMMON SNIPE:

There are people who believe the snipe is an imaginary bird, made up to trick new arrivals to summer camps into the infamous snipe hunt. Not only is the snipe real, but it is frequently heard, though not often recognized, in marshy fields throughout

In flight, these big birds can be distinguished from Canada geese by their longer neck and legs. On the ground, the only other bird with which it might be confused is the great blue heron, which in Alaska tends to be more grayish than blue. However, an adult sandhill crane will have a bright red patch on its crown that is usually quite visible. Also, unlike herons, cranes will often be in large flocks, numbering in the hundreds during migration. In fall, watch for migrating cranes flying

along north flanks of the Alaska Range in Denali National Park.

SEMIPALMATED PLOVER:

Plovers are compact birds that like to race across tidal flats and along riverbanks. One of the smallest plovers is the semi-palmated. The term refers to the partial webbing between its toes, a feature that is not easily determined in the field. What is distinctive in the field is a white collar around its neck with a broad, dark brown

early summer. As part of its mating ritual, the male snipe will fly high, then spread its tail feathers while free falling to the ground. The wind through the feathers creates a rapid hooting sound. The common snipe is a mottled brown shorebird with short legs and a long bill. It is well-camouflaged, making it difficult to see when hidden in grass. If you approach too close, it will quickly take off in a beeline flight. Before it gets too far away, you may notice tan stripes down the length of its body.

BONAPARTE'S GULL:

The Bonaparte's gull is one of those "seagulls" that is often seen far from any sea. One of the smallest gulls, the Bonaparte's is fairly common throughout Alaska except for the North Slope. Breeding adults have a white body with gray wings, a distinctive black head and bill, and orange-red legs. Some other gulls have black heads but they are rare in Alaska, so spotting a Bonaparte's might be worth a closer look. In winter and juvenile plumage, the Bonaparte's has a mostly white head with a black spot behind the eyes, similar to a black-legged kittiwake.

Spines on the end of the common snipe's long tongue and serrations on its upper mandible enable it to move worms and crane-fly larvae up its long bill and down its gullet. (James L. Davis)

TREE AND VIOLET-GREEN SWALLOWS:

When the swallows come back to Alaska, you know it's mosquito season again. Tree swallows, and the other species of swallows found in Alaska, are voracious mosquito eaters. A small bird swooping through open areas is likely to be a swallow feeding on insects. The question is, which swallow is it? Tree and violet-green swallows inhabit the same areas and sport similar plumage, a creamy white belly with a glossy greenish-blue body and wings. The most obvious difference during flight is that the violet-green swallow has a white patch that extends from its belly onto its rump. Once you get used to looking for this patch, it is quite noticeable. The violet-green also has a white patch that curls around its eye, but this is better seen when the bird is perched.

VARIED THRUSH:

One of the first songbirds to return in the spring to Alaska's forested areas, the varied thrush usually perches on the top of a tall conifer, which makes for difficult

Coniferous forests near lakes and ponds are favored nesting grounds for Bonaparte's gulls. In winter or during migration, they're often found on tidal flats, beaches, and marine estuaries, their flight patterns resembling those of terns more so than other gulls. (Jon R. Nickles)

viewing in places like Southeast where mature trees are well over 100 feet high. But its unique, drawn out, one note song simplifies identification. If you get to see the varied thrush, it is one of the easier thrushes to identify. It's about the size and shape of a robin (also a thrush) with a dark-orange-colored breast. Both male and female have a black bar across the top of the breast; the bar is more noticeable on males.

ORANGE-CROWNED WARBLER:

One of the most common warblers in Alaska, the orange-crowned's distinction is that it has none. While most birds have some identifying field mark, the orange-crowned is uniformly greenish-yellow with no wing bars, different tail feathers, or anything else. Males do have a bright orange crown, but this is seldom visible. The best way to identify this bird is by its song. But even this isn't foolproof, since it closely resembles that of a dark-eyed junco.

GOLDEN-CROWNED SPARROW:

One of the more common sparrows in Alaska, particularly in shrubby areas near

ABOVE: *Well-adapted to aerial life, swallows spend more time in daylight flight than other songbird species found in Alaska. This tree swallow was caught resting for a moment on a spring branch at Potter Marsh near Anchorage. Tree and violet-green swallows can be distinguished by the white that extends above the eye and part way across the rump of the violet-green swallow. (Harry M. Walker)*

ABOVE RIGHT: *With a beakful of bugs, a varied thrush pauses beside a lakeshore on the Kenai Peninsula. Its diet also includes worms, seeds, and berries. (Loren Taft/Alaskan Images)*

treeline, the golden-crowned sparrow has a golden-colored stripe on the top of its head that is bordered by a black band. Other than a grayish face, the rest of the bird is mostly brown, like most sparrows. Sitting on the top of a shrub, the golden-crowned belts out an easily identifiable, three-note song, "oh dear me."

WHITE-WINGED CROSSBILL:

The male is pink and the female is yellowish-gray, similar to the male and female pine grosbeak. Also, both species are found in coniferous forests throughout Alaska. White-winged crossbills, however, have two distinct white wing bars and are about two-thirds the size of a grosbeak. The wing bars on the pine grosbeak are fairly drab. If you get close enough, you will see that the curvature of the crossbill's bill is more exaggerated than that of the grosbeak. In winter, crossbills travel in large flocks, whereas pine grosbeak flocks usually contain just a few birds.

Roosting on a Radar Tower

By Elizabeth Manning

EDITOR'S NOTE: *Elizabeth Manning writes for the* Anchorage Daily News, *covering wildlife and conservation. In summer of 2000, she traveled to Middleton Island.*

Imagine tufted puffins burrowed in ship toilets. Hundreds of black-legged kittiwakes squawking in a wide halo around an abandoned U.S. Air Force radar tower. Or common murres, those slender black-and-white seabirds, packed together on a building shelf as if socializing at a cocktail party, listening to a recording of other murres' chattering as part of an experiment to jumpstart a new colony.

It all exists — in the Gulf of Alaska on Middleton Island, 80 miles southwest of Cordova. Remote Middleton, mostly flat and definitely solitary, is the state's most unusual laboratory for studying seabirds. Biologists study several seabird species here: common and thick-billed murres, tufted puffins, black-legged kittiwakes, plus glaucous-winged gulls, pelagic cormorants, and rhinoceros auklets.

Once a Cold War outpost, Middleton is now mainly a biology research station run by the U.S. Geological Survey and a weather observation facility run by the Federal Aviation Administration. Scott Hatch, a seabird biologist with USGS's Alaska Biological Science Center, is the lead researcher. Since the mid 1980s, he and a team of seabird biologists have spent part or all of nearly every summer on Middleton, drawn there by the unparalleled access to seabirds.

The unusual proximity comes from the strange places the birds use for nesting. In addition to hatching and rearing their young on cliff faces, the most typical habitat of these small gulls, black-legged kittiwakes have also flocked to Middleton's abandoned buildings and structures, such as the old radar tower, military barracks, or the USS *Coldbrook*, a merchant marine vessel grounded on the island in the mid 1940s.

From beneath the tower, one hears a constant, high-pitched chorus of screeches and sees a sky filled with the flurry of hundreds of beating, black-tipped, white wings. Enter the tower and the smell is of salt, old fish, must, feathers, and bird droppings, a smell that is both acidic and sweet, overpowering at first but surprisingly easy to get used to. The biologists spend weeks wearing the same unwashed, slick green coveralls.

The work that Hatch and his colleagues have done on Middleton Island is similar to other seabird research throughout the state with one exception: Because of the

LEFT: *From inside the tower, a black-legged kittiwake and chicks are observed on their nest. Biologists have banded many birds here to discover more about the species' habits. (Elizabeth Manning,* Anchorage Daily News)

FACING PAGE: *Scientists noticed seabirds nesting on this old Air Force tower on Middleton Island in the mid 1980s and turned it into a bird research laboratory. (Elizabeth Manning,* Anchorage Daily News)

Grounded for nearly 60 years on the coast of Middleton Island, the USS Coldbrook *accommodates hundreds of black-legged kittiwake nests. (Elizabeth Manning,* Anchorage Daily News*)*

island's unique nesting spots, the biologists can experiment with the birds instead of just observe them.

Hatch once placed scales beneath some of the kittiwake nests crowded on the decks of the USS *Coldbrook* so he could weigh the birds as they hatched and then reared their young. The ship is like a bird condominium. Birds line the steel I-beams and pack themselves especially close together on the front deck, which looks like an oasis, with grass growing in big, luscious green clumps on top of the rusted brown-red metal. One kittiwake nests on a ship's pulley, gently swinging in the breeze.

To peer into the dark homes of the puffins and the auklets, the biologists use what they call a "burrow cam," a small remote camera attached to the end of a hoselike cord. Sometimes, the biologists also wait in ambush in the salmonberry bushes for auklets to return to their burrows, startling them with nets as they scurry up from the beach, forcing the birds to drop their bill-load of food. The biologists do this so they can learn exactly what the birds eat and how much.

In one of his studies, Hatch and his researchers fed birds on the radar tower to see how the food they eat affects nesting success. They can do this because the tower is retrofitted with hundreds of panels of one-way glass that can be removed to pull the kittiwakes inside for closer study. Whenever biologists need to weigh, measure, or band a bird, they simply slip a wire hook through a slot beneath each window and loop it around the bird's leg. Then they lift the one-way window and snatch the bird inside. Minutes later, the bird is released through a hatch in the wall, and it usually settles back on its nest quickly, as if nothing happened.

The results of Hatch's studies are dramatic: The birds that nest on the island's cliffs, which ring the mostly flat island and drop down a few hundred feet to sea level, have had almost no success raising young.

"Middleton was probably the world's largest kittiwake colony at one time, but it's undergone a drastic decline," Hatch said. "The birds on the cliffs have chronic and abject reproductive failure."

In contrast, birds living on the tower that get fed have an average success rate of about one chick per nesting pair, and unfed birds on the tower have also started to raise young again. In essence, the biologists have rescued the kittiwake colony on the tower.

"Once a few birds start getting their act together and raising their young, everyone gets their act together," Hatch said. "Today it's becoming a functional colony again rather than a dysfunctional one."

But elsewhere on the island, kittiwake numbers have continued to decline. Around 1980, Middleton supported 160,000 kittiwakes. Today, the island is home to fewer than 20,000 of the small gulls. Hatch thinks the main reason is food. Because of changing winds, currents, and weather in the Gulf of Alaska — the same regime shift that may be responsible for the decline of Steller sea lions — the fat-rich fish that kittiwakes

depend on have declined, while pollock, a leaner fish with less nutritional value for seabirds, have increased.

"Some foods are like fat juicy steaks while others are like McDonald's hamburgers," said Rick Lanctot, another seabird researcher who has worked with Hatch on Middleton.

But that may be changing. This past summer, Hatch said kittiwakes "turned up their noses" at the fatty capelin that his crew fed the birds through plastic tubes stuck through the walls. Instead, the birds appeared to have no problem finding their own high-quality food in the ocean, he said, which might prove to be an early indication of another regime shift.

"That's what we're starting to see," Hatch said. "And now we have a lot of baseline data with which to document the change as it occurs."

Bristle-thighed curlews stop at Middleton Island on their long-distance migration over the Pacific Ocean. These shorebirds eat crustaceans, mollusks, berries, and as shown here, an occasional sand lance. They exhibit a habit rare among shorebirds — they'll eat other bird's eggs. (Lon E. Lauber)

But there are always complications, especially when it comes to understanding habitats and natural cycles of change. During the 1964 earthquake, Middleton lurched upwards a few feet from the ocean floor, altering the nature of the cliffs that once dropped right down into the ocean. This has made the cliffs less suitable nesting habitat for kittiwakes and murres. The murres must now cross long stretches of brackish meadowland in some places to reach the ocean that was once right beneath the

cliffs, and for the kittiwakes, the cliffs have lost the sheer faces that once protected them from predation by gulls.

Verena Gill, another Middleton researcher, said she fears that one day the kittiwakes may disappear, even from the tower, which is today a thriving colony.

"It may be too late for the birds on Middleton," she said. "One day we may go out there and they will all be gone."

Imagine how silent the skies will seem then. •

"How can that small bird survive these harsh conditions?" I wondered. In early December my friend Joe and I were on a skiing trip, exploring the solitude settling on Beaver Creek northwest of Fairbanks. We were striding along on the frozen creek in the zero degree cold when the dark gray bird popped out of a steamy hole in the ice where water gurgled just below. As the bird flew downstream, we recognized it as an American dipper, a waterproof songbird that lives in fast-flowing streams and remains at its home stream throughout the year, even though ice may severely restrict its available habitat. I have since observed that dippers, formerly known as water ouzels, will hang out underneath shelf ice that forms around shallow rapids. It's warmer there than in the frigid air above and air pockets allow the dipper to forage for aquatic insects buried in the gravel. It's a niche the dipper has all to itself.

Winter in Alaska lasts a long time, typically five to seven months, requiring more fortitude than just enduring an occasional winter storm. If the climate in a particular

FACING PAGE: *Flightless until about 30 days old, a mew gull chick cries for its parent who will offer the young bird regurgitated food held in the tip of its own beak or deposited on the ground. (Jon R. Nickles)*

Secrets of Survival

By George Matz

region is not extremely cold, then it is extremely wet, with heavy accumulations of snow mixed with rain. Coastal storms unleash hurricane force winds. Long hours of darkness limit foraging time. Of the 264 species of birds that breed in Alaska, less than 60 species stick it out through winter. Because so many leave Alaska before winter sets in, those species that stay have less competition for available habitat. But survival depends on being able to adapt to Alaska's challenging conditions.

Birds that overwinter can survive incredibly cold conditions if they have enough food. And food for virtually all wildlife begins with plant growth. The energy captured by plants during the summer gets converted to seeds and berrylike fruits during fall. These seeds and berries supply food throughout the winter for species that are able to take advantage of their nutrition,

like common redpolls and bohemian waxwings.

Luxuriant plant growth during summer also contributes to Alaska's abundance of insects. As summer progresses, insects lay eggs that turn into larvae and then pupae, an inactive stage in an insect's life cycle. Insects typically wait out winter as pupae. Spiders also lay eggs, suspending life until spring. Eggs, larvae, and pupae laid in the bark of trees are an accessible source of food for birds.

But surviving the winter requires more than specialized feeding techniques to stoke their high-energy metabolisms. Bodies, like houses, need not only a good furnace to keep warm, but also some means to retain the heat. Birds that successfully survive Alaska's winters have developed morphological, physiological, and behavioral adaptations that conserve energy. Without

ABOVE: *The American dipper is one of few year-round birds at Old John Lake, near Arctic Village in the Arctic National Wildlife Refuge. Long toes built for grasping rocks allow them to forage completely submerged in fast-flowing streams. (David Roseneau)*

ABOVE RIGHT: *Even when the mercury dips below freezing in the Interior, the black-backed woodpecker remains, probing under the bark of dead trees for insects and larvae. About 75 percent of its food consists of destructive spruce bark beetles, responsible for the slow death of millions of older spruce trees around the state in recent years. (James L. Davis)*

these adaptations, birds would have difficulty consuming enough food to stay warm.

Foraging Adaptations

The diet for any species of bird depends on its preferred habitat and its food gathering adaptations. These factors have been used to group birds into ecological categories. While this approach compared to the more familiar taxonomic classifications may seem confusing, birds in the same family tend to have similar ecosystem requirements and food gathering adaptations. Ecological categories include seabirds, coastal and interior waterbirds, carnivores and scavengers, insectivores, granivores (seed-eating), frugivores (fruit-eating), nectarivores, and an "other" group, primarily ground-dwellers like grouse and ptarmigan. Although all these categories are represented by birds that breed in Alaska, not all are suitable to Alaska's winters. Let's take a look at those that are.

Mainland Alaska winter birds include few seabirds or waterbirds. Seabirds, such as puffins, nest in coastal areas during the summer but are usually far offshore during winter. Waterbirds feed on or in the water; examples are loons, grebes, ducks, geese, swans, gulls, terns, shorebirds. To enhance their ability to forage in, on, or near the water, ducks have webbed feet and a broad, flat bill designed for straining or grasping food. The length of the legs and the length and shape of the bill define a shorebird's place on the mudflats. Birds with longer bills, like godwits, probe deeper, feeding on different invertebrates than a shorter-billed sanderling or western sandpiper.

Since waterbirds require open water, most migrate south for winter. However, for loons and many diving ducks such as mergansers, scoters, goldeneyes, buffleheads, oldsquaw, and harlequin, the open waters of coastal Southcentral and Southeast are far enough. Here rafts of seaducks feed on small fish, crustaceans, and mollusks. I have seen rafts with thousands of scoters in Lynn Canal. Some of the diving ducks, mostly mallards, will overwinter where there is open fresh water and adequate food, usually near human settlement where warm effluents keep water from freezing and people provide food. Mallards did not appear on Anchorage Audubon Society's Christmas Bird Count list until 1970. By 1982, they had become one of the most numerous species, hitting a high of 3,351 ducks in 1996. Gulls, in adapting to ever-growing mounds of human garbage throughout the world, have learned to include garbage dumps on their shopping list. When garbage is plentiful, gulls can tolerate cold weather. Anchorage's Merrill Field used to have an open dump where glaucous-winged gulls were common during the winter. Now that the dump is closed, gulls no longer appear on the Anchorage CBC list.

Despite generally frozen conditions, bird-watchers can expect to see a few shorebird species, notably rock sandpipers during the winter in open coastal waters. Most can be found in rocky, intertidal areas where mollusks are exposed at low tide. More than 20,000 rock sandpipers overwinter at the mouth of the Susitna River where icebergs, moved by the tide, gouge into the beach and expose small clams.

Year-round resident carnivorous birds include hawks, falcons, eagles, owls, and the northern shrike. These birds are well-equipped to be predators. Their binocular vision enables them to see prey at long distances and their flying abilities have adapted to their style of hunting. Accipiters, like the sharp-shinned hawk and northern goshawk, are fast and mobile, allowing them to dodge trees as they pursue forest songbirds. Falcons, such as the peregrine and gyrfalcon, have streamlined shapes and powerful, fast flight. They launch stunning attacks on birds and small mammals, sometimes knocking waterfowl out of the sky. The buteos, though not winter residents, are broad-winged hawks that soar effortlessly while scanning for small mammals. Owls have excellent low-light vision and pinpoint directional hearing, making night-hunting their niche. All these species have sharp talons for a deadly grip and strong, curved beaks for tearing the flesh of their victims or carrion.

The sexes are outwardly alike in rock sandpipers, with the female slightly larger than the male. Like most wading birds, they have short tails. (Lon E. Lauber)

The carnivorous species a bird-watcher can expect to see during the winter depends on what food is available. Since some fish inhabit coastal waters all winter, many bald eagles remain in Alaska, but they concentrate in areas with late-run salmon, such as the Chilkat River near Haines, or around fish-processing plants. A few golden eagles find enough prey or carrion to survive winter in the Alaska Range. The northern goshawk, gyrfalcon, and owls — typically the great horned, great gray, boreal, and northern hawk owl — catch small mammals such as voles, red squirrels, and snowshoe hares, and birds. These prey species can be found throughout Alaska in the winter and so can carnivorous birds, although sightings are not common. Hare and lemming populations undergo cycles. During low population years, carnivorous birds must migrate far in search of better hunting. This movement is called an irruptive migration, which happens most notably when snowy owls leave the Arctic and show up as far south as the northern tier states.

*Ravens (*Corvus corax*) are expert scavengers, but they also kill small animals, such as this squirrel, for food, sometimes caching scraps and returning later to eat them. (Tom Walker)*

Insectivores catch insects in a variety of ways. Some, like swallows, have wide mouths to snatch insects out of the air while flying. Although swallows prefer open areas, I have watched them from my deck fly full speed right into a thicket of birch and alder and, much to my amazement, come out the other side unscathed. Flycatchers catch insects by darting from a perch and grabbing their prey on the wing. Other insectivores are nocturnal or ground specialists. Since winter's cold curtails the activities of most insects, the types of insectivores found in Alaska at this time are bark- and tree-gleaning specialists.

Songbirds that forage under bark have strong feet and sharp claws that enable them to cling like lumberjacks to the sides of trees. They use their thin bills to probe the bark, looking for spiders and insect eggs, larvae, and pupae. In Southcentral and Southeast Alaska, the brown creeper and red-breasted nuthatch represent this group. These species often mix with flocks of chickadees. The old saying about safety in numbers may explain why songbirds sometimes forage in mixed flocks. More birds mean more eyes to detect predators and more numbers helps confuse an attacker. Being in a group also allows a bird to spend more time feeding and less watching for danger.

Woodpeckers are the most obvious bark specialists. Their strong claws and stiff tail are well-suited to clinging in trees. The impact-cushioning design of the beak and skull allows them to drill deep into the tree where they probe beneath the bark with their long, hinged tongue to capture insect larvae and pupae. Hairy, downy, three-toed, and black-backed woodpeckers reside year-round in most of the state's forested areas. These birds help curtail insect infestations, such as that of the spruce bark beetle. Biologists have estimated that one black-backed woodpecker eats 13,500 beetle larvae annually.

Walk in the forest on any calm winter day for a look at tree-gleaners foraging through the needles of conifers and the branches of birch and other hardwoods. Gleaners include chickadees, one of Alaska's most common winter species; golden-crowned kinglets in Southcentral and Southeast; and winter wrens in Southeast. Most insectivores that are year-round residents feed on seeds wedged in spruce cones and on birch and alder catkins in winter. Birds that feed mostly on seeds during

winter, such as sparrows, have short, conical bills for cracking open the protective hulls.

Alaska abounds in berry shrubs but has few fruit trees. Low-lying shrubs are often buried under snow much of the winter and are not accessible to most birds. Consequently, during winter there isn't much food for the common frugivores, like thrushes, which migrate to warmer climes. Three fruit-eating species that remain are

A merlin in Denali National Park eats a white-crowned sparrow it caught in flight, the characteristic tactic used by this member of the falcon family. When hunting, merlins usually fly low to the ground. (Patrick J. Endres)

the pine grosbeak, white-winged crossbill, and bohemian waxwing. The grosbeak and crossbill switch from eating berries and

Though approximately 220,000 Steller's eiders exist, mostly in Russia, sightings are now rare in Alaska. Few nests have been found since the mid 1970s on the Yukon-Kuskokwim Delta, once the most abundant breeding site in the state. In 1997, scientists estimated there were only about 1,000 breeding pairs, confined mainly to the North Slope, and officially deemed the species threatened. (Tom Soucek)

wings arrive. The state's native mountain ash is a shrub with limited berry production. However, in urban Alaska the larger European mountain ash has become a popular ornamental tree and has significantly increased the supply of winter food for waxwings. On the Anchorage CBC, waxwing numbers have increased from in the hundreds in the 1960s and 1970s to thousands during the past several years. In 2000, the highest count yet, more than 9,800 were tallied.

Nectar-eating birds survive by extracting the sweet liquid from flowers using long bills; some have a tubular tongue that essentially acts as a straw. These birds usually inhabit the tropics and sub-tropics where flowers bloom throughout the year. Although the rufous hummingbird is one nectarivore that is reasonably common in Southeast and in the Prince William Sound area during summer, it does not overwinter in Alaska.

The "other" category in this ecological classification includes some species that are important residents: grouse, ptarmigan, and the corvids: jays, magpies, crows, and ravens. Blue and spruce grouse live in coniferous forests where the bulk of their winter diet is needles. Ruffed grouse inhabit mixed deciduous/coniferous forests and have a more varied diet. Corvids are omnivorous, devouring just about any edible plant or animal matter. Gray and Steller's jays and black-billed magpies

buds to conifer seeds. Both species have what look like deformed bills but these curved beaks actually enable them to pull seeds out of cones.

During winter, large flocks of bohemian waxwings congregate around trees with fruits and berries. One of their favorites is the mountain ash, which keeps its small, red berries all winter, or at least until the wax-

are easily attracted to feeders.

Winter bird survival hinges on food storage as well as availability. Chickadees and nuthatches store seeds in tree crevasses, assuring a food supply every day even if bad weather limits their foraging. Jays are known to have a highly developed sense of spatial recognition and can actually remember for months where they cached food. In aviary studies where nuts buried by jays were either moved or some landmark was altered, the birds became confused and were unable to find their caches.

With about 20 hours of darkness in much of Alaska during midwinter, the long night can be as threatening as cold temperatures. To fend off cold, small birds in particular may need to be stoked with more fuel, even before daylight breaks and foraging can resume. Common and hoary redpolls have developed an enlarged esophagus to store seeds overnight. Each night as their energy begins to wane, they bring up these seeds for a much-needed snack. Ptarmigan have a similar ability.

Conserving Body Heat

In addition to developing feeding mechanisms that allow birds to live off a limited food supply, winter residents have other adaptations to contend with the cold. Like energy conservation measures in our homes, these adaptations reduce the amount of fuel birds need to be comfortable and, as a result, the amount of time they need to forage.

BELOW: *White-winged crossbills are attracted to "salt licks," and can sometimes be seen pecking the ground beside salted roadways. (Tom Walker)*

RIGHT: *The long tail of the male oldsquaw distinguishes it from the female. Its genus name,* Clangula, *is Latin for "clangor," naming the oldsquaw as one of the noisiest of all ducks. Many of Alaska's nesting oldsquaws winter in the Bering Sea. (Gary Schultz)*

Chickadee Bill Deformities: An Epidemic

By Colleen Handel

EDITOR'S NOTE: *Colleen Handel is a biologist with the Alaska Biological Science Center of the U.S. Geological Survey in Anchorage. She has researched landbirds and shorebirds for 25 years in Alaska, and since 1998, has studied the phenomenon of deformed beaks in chickadee populations here.*

Black-capped chickadees are small, resident songbirds that brighten dreary Alaska winter days with their cheerful "chick-a-dee" calls as they search in flocks for birch catkins, insects hidden in bark crevices, and sunflower seeds at residential feeders. They are among the first to signal the coming of spring with their lilting, bell-like "fee-bee" songs. Alarmingly high numbers of these delightful birds, however, have

Black-capped chickadees captured in January 1998 reveal the difference between a normal bird (left) and one with a deformed bill. Other bird species in Alaska have been recorded with the same defect, though scientists aren't sure yet what's causing the malady. (Colleen Handel, USGS Alaska Biological Science Center)

recently been appearing throughout Alaska with grossly deformed bills. As of June 2000, almost 600 sightings of deformed chickadees, representing at least 475 different individuals, have been reported. In addition, about 100 individuals of 18 other species of birds have been observed in Alaska with similar bill deformities. These include many year-round residents such as

nuthatches, woodpeckers, jays, and magpies as well as several species that migrate south for the winter, like the yellow-rumped warbler and savannah sparrow.

The bill deformities can be quite variable, ranging from hardly noticeable to extremely grotesque. Generally, the upper mandible is elongated and curved downward. In one individual, the bill was so

long that it almost pierced the bird's own breast. Several people who have seen deformed chickadees initially thought the birds were carrying long, skinny black twigs in their bills. The lower mandible is often normal, but sometimes it can be elongated and curved upward. The mandibles are often crossed, sometimes quite severely.

The earliest records of chickadee bill deformities in Alaska are from 1991, when two birds were observed in the Matanuska Valley and two were seen in the Bristol Bay area. Since then the number of reports has increased dramatically, with 78 reports from winter 1997-1998, 209 from 1998-1999, and 251 from 1999-2000. New observations continue to be reported. By comparison, only eight records of black-capped chickadees with abnormal bills have been reported from the rest of North America combined, all of which are records of single birds in different places and different years dating back to 1986.

In Alaska, most of the reports of birds with bill deformities are clustered in Southcentral, primarily in the Matanuska Valley, Anchorage, and Eagle River areas. Reports come regularly from as far north as Talkeetna, east to Cordova, and south to Homer. There is a small cluster reported from King Salmon, Naknek, and Dillingham in the Bristol Bay region. Only a few reports have been from outside this area, ranging from the Colville River on the North Slope, east to the Canadian border, down to Southeast Alaska, and west to the Aleutian Islands. Most of the reports have come from people with residential bird feeders, so it is unknown how many deformed birds may be occurring away from urban areas but are just not being seen.

Reports of sightings are usually

In Petersburg, a chestnut-backed chickadee with a normal bill visits a feeder. Birds with deformed bills have difficulty grasping seeds and other small bits of food, and may die prematurely due to starvation. (Don Cornelius)

from feeders during the winter, which is when they are most easily observed at close range. Chickadees with deformed bills have great difficulty feeding. Once the bill gets too long, the birds can no longer peck sunflower seeds open to extract the meat. They rely on softer foods such as peanut butter and suet. Birds with extremely long bills are often seen

feeding on the ground underneath feeders with their heads turned sideways to pick up pieces of fallen suet. Birds have trouble preening their feathers and by late winter their plumage is matted and disheveled. Few of these deformed birds probably manage to survive long, since they are susceptible to predators and hypothermia.

Many factors can cause such bill

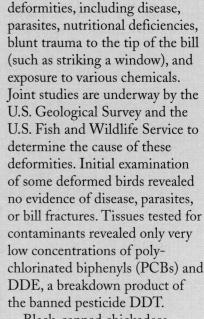

deformities, including disease, parasites, nutritional deficiencies, blunt trauma to the tip of the bill (such as striking a window), and exposure to various chemicals. Joint studies are underway by the U.S. Geological Survey and the U.S. Fish and Wildlife Service to determine the cause of these deformities. Initial examination of some deformed birds revealed no evidence of disease, parasites, or bill fractures. Tissues tested for contaminants revealed only very low concentrations of polychlorinated biphenyls (PCBs) and DDE, a breakdown product of the banned pesticide DDT.

Black-capped chickadees and many of the other afflicted species remain in Alaska all year, so whatever is causing these deformities is local in origin. Alaskans have been helping immensely in the efforts to find the cause. People throughout the state report sightings of deformed birds at their feeders and residents in Southcentral have put up nest boxes in their backyards so that researchers can examine eggs and nestlings for evidence of abnormalities. Such concerted efforts should help assure that the lilting song of the chickadee continues to signal the onset of spring. •

Some ecological rules generally describe how birds and mammals adapt their body size, shape, and color to climatic conditions. According to Bergmann's Rule, colder climates tend to have larger animals than warmer climates. Larger size aids survival because of the higher ratio of body size to surface area. Body mass generates heat and surface area loses it. This rule generally works when applied to populations within a species, but not between species. For instance, many songbirds that breed in Alaska and migrate south are larger than the black-capped chickadee that stays here. But within the species, black-capped chickadees from Washington state are smaller than those from the Fairbanks area. Black-capped chickadees captured in Washington and released in Fairbanks during the winter not only weighed less on average, but the smallest ones did not survive. Those that did were about the same weight as an average Fairbanks chickadee.

Allen's Rule states that animals living in colder climates have proportionately shorter appendages. Long appendages have more surface area that drains vital body heat. While the applicability of this rule is debated, field guides sometimes describe

Despite subzero temperatures, mallards often remain in Alaska through the winter, inhabiting patches of open water in urban areas in southern coastal regions. (Lon E. Lauber)

RIGHT: *Alaska's gulls have learned to scavenge food from humans. Fishing boats and canneries, as well as landfills, trash bins, and campgrounds offer prime pickings for these resourceful birds. (Lon E. Lauber)*

FAR RIGHT: *Like white leaves, a flock of snow buntings perch on cottonwood branches in the Matanuska Valley. Snow buntings are able to withstand temperatures approaching minus 60 degrees F, but they will burrow into snow for insulation. (Don Cornelius)*

the differences between geographically dispersed species of the same family by the length of certain appendages. The hoary redpoll, a finch that winters in the Arctic and Interior, has a "slightly smaller bill" than the common redpoll, which winters in the Interior and Southcentral. The bill length of other finches varies accordingly, with those from colder climates having shorter bills.

Gloger's Rule applies to temperature and humidity. Birds that inhabit warm, humid climates have darker plumage than those that reside in cold or dry areas. A study of 52 North American bird species found that 50 conform to this rule. Many birds of the Arctic have light-colored or nearly all-white plumage with no pigment in their feathers, like snowy owls and winter-plumaged ptarmigan. Biologists speculate that the cost of producing pigments is too high where life is already marginal. Also, white

feathers may reflect more solar radiation closer to the skin where the heat is most needed. But nothing is certain and there are notable exceptions such as the raven.

Plumage is the most important body structure birds have for fending off winter discomfort. An intricate combination of feathers and down not only insulates birds from the cold but also keeps them dry and blocks wind chill. Without reminders from fashion catalogs, birds molt their feathers throughout the year to have the proper attire for the season. As winter approaches, birds in colder climates add more feathers, as much as 70 percent in the case of some sparrows. Small birds like chickadees, creepers, and kinglets have a greater density of feathers than larger birds. Feathers amount

to about 10 to 11 percent of the body weight of these small birds, compared to only 6 to 8 percent of larger birds. When it gets really cold, birds have other strategies. Ever notice how birds look bigger when it gets colder? That's because they puff out their feathers to create bigger air pockets, thereby increasing their amount of insulation.

Birds have few fleshy parts exposed to the cold. The unfeathered parts of their legs are mostly bone and tendons and their beaks are made of skeletal material. They also add

Feathered legs and feet help keep the white-tailed ptarmigan warm through the winter. Acting as "snowshoes," the feathers buoy the bird on the top layer of snow as it forages for twigs and leaves. (Jon R. Nickles)

heats the returning venous blood, which would otherwise cool their body. When it gets really cold, ducks retract one leg into the protection of their plumage and stand on the other for long periods of time.

Behavior can be another defense against the cold. Birds that use tree cavities huddle together at night, sharing lost body heat. Ptarmigan and grouse plunge into powder snow, sometimes staying in their snow cave for days when it is extremely cold. Like people, birds favor areas that have more sunlight, as weak as it is, and less wind chill; something to remember when you are deciding where to put a feeder.

Advantages to Resident Birds

Winter does take its toll, even on species that are well-adapted to Alaska's extremes. It is not unusual for half the juveniles of a clutch to perish before winter softens into spring. But birds that survive have an advantage when it comes to breeding. First of all, they do not have to spend energy migrating to Alaska. This leaves them in better shape to begin breeding. They do not suffer the significant mortality from storms, predation, and man-made hazards during

fat before the winter that not only insulates their warm body but provides a ready source of fuel. Some small songbirds will eat enough during the day to add as much as 15 percent to their body weight in fat, which is then burned off during the night. Many species lower their body temperature and energy needs at night. Black-capped chickadees reduce their body temperature by as much as 18 degrees F, lowering their metabolic rate by as much as 23 percent. Shivering is another way birds and

mammals keep warm because it releases metabolic energy that becomes heat.

Have you ever watched ducks and geese stand barefooted on ice for hours and wonder how they do it? These waterbirds, as well as some wading birds, restrict blood flow to their legs, thereby reducing heat loss. They also have a complex circulatory network in their legs that keeps cold feet from chilling their core temperature. The arteries and veins in their legs are intertwined so that the warm arterial blood

migration. An increasingly serious hazard for migrating birds is collision with man-made structures such as building windows and transmission towers. Experts estimate that about 100 million birds die each year from collisions with buildings and skyscrapers just in the United States and Canada. The U.S. Fish and Wildlife Service speculates that as many as 40 million are killed every year by hitting transmission towers.

Another advantage for non-migratory birds is that they get first pick at nesting sites. These hardy survivors start laying eggs before most migrants even begin returning. With many species, eggs start hatching about the same time temperatures creep above freezing. This coincides with the hatching of many insects, assuring an abundant source of food for the young. Like the old cliché about the early bird getting the worm, this early source of food gives resident songbirds a head start in raising their family. It also gives them a fallback if there should be predation or a late return of winter that kills the eggs or hatchlings.

A pair of greater white-fronted geese marches through a marsh at Hartney Bay, near Cordova, during their yearly migration in May. Vast numbers of birds pass through this area every spring, and in their honor, the Copper River Delta Shorebird Festival was started in 1990. (Mike Jones)

Because of their early start, they still have enough time to lay a second clutch and raise the young before winter sets in.

To illustrate the early start, let's look at ravens, one of the first resident species to begin breeding. Courtship behavior begins in mid January. By mid March adult pairs are roosting near their nesting site, usually a cliff or tall conifer. The female lays from three to seven eggs in a nest that looks like a basket of twigs and small branches. Only the female incubates the eggs but the male feeds her. Chicks hatch after about three weeks, grow quickly, and leave the nest about four weeks after hatching.

There are thousands of species of birds, each with its own strategy on how to survive and how to pass on its genes to another generation. While the goals may be simple, achieving them is complex. This creates an infinite opportunity to learn more about the wondrous workings of nature. While the number of species is just a fraction of the world's animal species inventory, birds are among the most obvious and easy to observe. Learning about them not only increases our understanding of nature, but also the nature of ourselves.

An arctic fox prowls below a murre nest on St. Paul Island, hoping to capture chicks or eggs. (Hugh Rose)

Migration Pathways

By Brad A. Andres

EDITOR'S NOTE: *Brad A. Andres received his B.S. in Biology at Pennsylvania State University and later earned an M.S. and Ph.D. in Zoology from Ohio State University. He completed his master's and doctoral research in Alaska, where he concentrated on migrant shorebirds of the North Slope and breeding black oystercatchers in Prince William Sound. As a member of the U.S. Fish and Wildlife Service's Nongame Migratory Bird Management unit, he is involved in numerous projects concerning landbirds and shorebirds and helps coordinate monitoring efforts for these species groups in Alaska.*

Looking westward across the Gulf of Alaska from a beach near Yakutat, I am once again amazed by the phenomenal migrations of birds. It's May and tens, even hundreds, of thousands of birds are winging their way back to Alaska along North America's western coastline. Sandpipers, ducks, hawks, songbirds — right now you can find a representative of almost every type of bird that breeds in the state. Two weeks earlier, I had withstood cold, blustery winds at Gunsight Mountain to observe hundreds of hawks migrating through the Matanuska Valley near Anchorage. Anywhere you go in Alaska between late April and early June, you will be surrounded by hordes of migrant birds. Although Alaska does not support great numbers of species of breeding birds, no other spot in North America receives birds from as many flyways as does Alaska; in winter, birds that have bred here can be found on every continent. Many people have heard of the fantastic migration story of the arctic tern that breeds in Alaska and travels all the way to Antarctica to spend the winter. However, few realize that many of Alaska's birds migrate across vast distances each spring and fall. Long-distance migration is particularly prevalent among shorebirds and songbirds; some individuals in more than 55 percent of the species in these two groups cross the Tropic of Cancer to spend the winter. Alaska's migratory birds are truly an international resource.

This gray-crowned rosy-finch spotted in the Pribilof Islands is one of thousands of songbird species that follow the Pacific Flyway as the seasons turn. (Loren Taft/ Alaskan Images)

Following the Pacific Coast

There's nothing like seeing a group of 10,000 sandpipers crazily feeding on a mudflat to feel a part of a bird's world. Observing the spring migration of birds along the Pacific coast of Alaska is a great way to get connected. As the name implies, the Pacific Flyway is a migration corridor that lies along the west coast of North America. The coastline guides birds to and from Alaska. One of the most conspicuous bird groups to use this flyway is the shorebirds (plovers, sandpipers, curlews, oystercatchers, snipes, phalaropes, and turnstones). Many of these species form large flocks and concentrate in tidal estuaries during migration. Here they feed on worms, clams, and other invertebrates in mudflats exposed during low tide. After refueling at these "Stop-n-Gos," they are on their way. Because shorebirds concentrate in large numbers during migration, they are extremely vulnerable to catastrophic environmental disasters like oil spills. A program called the Western Hemisphere Shorebird

Reserve Network was launched by the Manomet Bird Observatory in eastern Massachusetts to identify areas where migratory birds concentrate and to work toward conservation of these areas. The program has identified 57 sites in Alaska that support more than 20,000 shorebirds during spring or fall migration.

One of the most abundant shorebirds on the Pacific coast is the western sandpiper. Beginning as far away as Ecuador, this small sandpiper that weighs about one ounce hopscotches along the coast back to its breeding grounds in western Alaska. Along the way, the

sandpiper flies 200 to 300 miles a day between estuaries. Leaving Ecuador, it stops in Panama, Honduras, Mexico, California, and British Columbia. On reaching Alaska, most westerns land at the Copper River Delta. Here in Southcentral Alaska, westerns spend about three days before continuing their migration. Biologists estimate that between five and eight million shorebirds, mostly western sandpipers, can be found on the Delta's mudflats each spring, making it one of the most important shorebird stopovers in the world.

Not all migratory birds choose

to refuel during their migration. Brant, small geese that breed on the tundra of western and northern Alaska, concentrate in large numbers in the fall at the western end of the Alaska Peninsula. When they have their fill of feeding on eelgrass, a rich estuarine plant, they fly non-stop across the Gulf of Alaska to the Pacific Northwest. Once landing along the coast there, many fly farther south to winter in the lagoons of western Baja California. Brant have no GPS units, compasses, or weather faxes to plan their journey or find their way. Yet year after year they make amazing long-distance, over-water flights. Biologists are only beginning to identify which species and how many individuals undertake long flights across the Gulf of Alaska. As the technology to follow small birds advances, biologists will likely discover that many songbirds embark on such fall migrations.

Waterfowl and shorebirds are not the only groups to use the Pacific Flyway. For six years, I have captured and banded songbirds a mile from the coast at Yakutat. During that period, our team captured more than 13,000 birds. Most of these birds nested somewhere south of the Alaska Range. An exhausted yellow warbler that

landed on a fishing boat offshore from Yakutat had been banded five days earlier on the central Alaska Peninsula. The birds we captured were on their way to many different spots to spend the winter: alder flycatchers to Peru; orange-crowned warblers to western Mexico; Lincoln's sparrows to Nicaragua; varied thrushes to Oregon; and golden-crowned sparrows to California. Even the rufous hummingbird, which can be found visiting feeders in Yakutat and weighs one-third ounce — the equivalent of a mere quarter-dollar — travels to the cloud forests of western Mexico to wait out Alaska's winter. Although all these species use the Pacific Flyway, they disembark at different points along the way. Alaska-breeding songbirds can be found in every country in Latin America between Peru and Mexico. They exist in all types of habitats from ornamental trees in city parks to pristine cloud forests. The breadth of their distribution and habitat use in the tropics makes generalizations about the

effects of habitat loss difficult, and biologists are only now gaining knowledge about the ecology of these birds on their wintering grounds.

Bending to the East

By 3:25 A.M., I am counting birds along a Breeding Bird Survey route at Lake Louise near Glennallen. For the next four and one-half hours, I will make 50 stops, for three minutes each, to

listen and look for birds — a ritual I perform each June. During the same month, people all over the country are undertaking similar rituals, making the Breeding Bird Survey the most widespread canvass for songbirds on the continent. I enjoy the Lake Louise route because I encounter a fair number of blackpoll warblers, the male of which is a striking black-and-white bird with a solid black cap. One of the things that intrigues me about

blackpolls is their migration strategy. In the fall, blackpolls do not follow the Pacific coast like songbirds at Yakutat but instead traverse the entire length of boreal Canada. Encountering the ocean along the coasts of New England and Maritime Canada, they stack up waiting for favorable weather. With passage of a northwesterly cold front that provides a tail wind, blackpolls take off for South America, eventually making land-

Arctic terns are an international, circumpolar species, nesting in arctic environs in countries from North America to Russia to Finland, then following flyways to Antarctica, a round trip of approximately 20,000 miles. (Tom Soucek)

fall in Suriname or Venezuela. Many of these small birds make this incredible journey non-stop, flying continuously for two days or more. Birds are able to store and use high energy fat reserves to make these flights. Migrant birds also take advantage of ideal weather conditions to reduce stress on their bodies. Although this appears to be an unusual migration route, a review of the breeding range of the blackpoll warbler might provide an explanation. At the end of the last ice age, about 10,000 years ago, blackpolls colonized northern North America from the east. Thus, their convoluted migration route is retracing their radiation across the continent.

Blackpoll warblers are not alone in following a migration path that bends to the east. Many of the songbirds that nest in interior Alaska follow the Rocky Mountains into Mexico and Central America. Some, like the Swainson's thrush, may cross the western Gulf of Mexico and continue to Panama and northern South America; others stop somewhere in the United States. The Smith's longspur, a sparrowlike bird that breeds in tundra along the Denali Highway and in the Brooks Range, spends the winter in grasslands of eastern Texas, eastern Oklahoma, and western Arkansas. Trailing the Swainson's thrush, the minute Wilson's warbler, one-quarter ounce, ends its journey in Guatemala. Here it shares the forest or shrublands with numerous resident bird species. Numbers of bird species found in tropical countries are much higher than in Alaska or North America. For example, in Panama (which is smaller than Oregon), about 950 species of birds have been recorded, more than has been recorded in all of the United States and Canada.

Other species besides blackpoll warblers migrate across large expanses of ocean. As early as 1492, Christopher Columbus noted a large migration of birds over the western Atlantic Ocean during the fall. Among this group of migrants was probably another Alaska-breeding bird, the American golden-plover. The golden-plover follows the blackpoll eastward and also refuels in wetlands along the Atlantic coast of North America. Like the blackpoll, it takes off from the North American coast and heads toward northern South America. Golden-plovers, however, are not content to remain on the beaches of Suriname or Venezuela. After refueling once again, the plovers continue to the pampas region of southern Brazil, Uruguay, and northern Argentina. Here they are joined by numerous shorebird species from the North Slope of Alaska: Baird's, buff-breasted, pectoral, and stilt sandpipers to name a few. In fact, of the 37 species of shorebirds that regularly breed in Alaska, some individuals of 28 species (76 percent) migrate to South America; many of these shorebird species

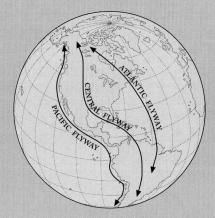

(ALASKA GEOGRAPHIC®
map by Kathy Doogan)

breed in the Arctic. To return to Alaska in the spring, shorebirds and songbirds follow a more westerly route through the center of the continent. Their route selection is mainly based on the direction and strength of prevailing winds. Weather and climate play a large role in the development of migration pathways for species and in the decisions of individuals on when to migrate. For example, northward movements of Canada geese are closely tied with decreasing amounts of snow cover at a particular latitude.

Across the Pacific Ocean

"A little more to the left," says Heather Johnson-Schultz, and I tweak the mist-net array one more time. We have spent the last week on the Colville River Delta, on Alaska's North Slope, trying to perfect ways to capture wary migrant dunlins. Our immediate objective is to lure dunlins into the nets, using repeated calls on a mini-CD, to place small green plastic flags on their legs. Our real purpose is to discover where North Slope-breeding dunlins spend the winter. About twice the size of a western sandpiper, the dunlin breeds on the tundra of western and northern Alaska. Birds breeding on the Yukon-Kuskokwim Delta follow the western sandpipers south along the Pacific coast, but dunlins nesting on the North Slope cross the Pacific Ocean to winter in estuaries in Japan, Korea, Taiwan, or China. On their wintering grounds, Alaska dunlins mix with Russian dunlins from Sakhalin Island, the Kamchatka Peninsula, and the Chukotka Peninsula. North Slope dunlins likely migrate along the coast of northwestern Alaska, fatten up on the mudflats of the Yukon-Kuskokwim Delta, and then head southwest across the Bering Sea. Because some populations may be declining, we need to sort out which dunlin populations are wintering where. Answering this question requires the cooperation of several countries.

Other species of waterfowl and shorebirds follow the dunlin's example. Northern pintails, ruddy turnstones, and black-bellied plovers can be observed in the wet-

A nylon stocking protects the feathers and gently restrains a trapped rough-legged hawk while it is weighed, measured, and banded. This hands-on method of learning about birds gives researchers a clearer understanding than does simple observation from afar. (David Roseneau)

lands of Japan during the winter. Western Alaska has a number of species that breed primarily in Russia. Most of these birds follow migration pathways that take them to wintering areas in Asia. The arctic warbler, a small, greenish, non-descript songbird, flies across the North Pacific to winter in the Philippines. Although the arctic warbler is found across northern Europe and Russia, only birds wintering in the Philippines travel to Alaska to breed. This information will help identify conservation strategies if biologists detect a decrease in the number of singing birds on Breeding Bird Survey routes in western Alaska. Without making these types of links,

scientists would not be able to effectively conserve populations of migratory birds.

I envy the large shorebirds that get to leave Alaska to winter along the beaches of South Pacific islands. I do not envy, however, the long over-water flights they must undertake to get to these warm destinations. When Pacific golden-plovers take off from the Alaska Peninsula, they have nowhere to land until they reach Hawaii, a distance of 2,400 miles. To accomplish such flights, shorebirds need to accumulate fat reserves of 50 to 100 percent of their body weight.

Following a similar pathway, some bristle-thighed curlews leaving the Yukon-Kuskokwim Delta

stop in the Hawaiian archipelago. However, many more fly several thousand additional miles to winter in Tahiti. This one-way, non-stop flight can total 5,000 miles. It's a mystery how a bird is able to predict weather patterns across those distances to ensure its survival. Scientific evidence indicates that young birds are not always successful in making the journey and many perish at sea. Because the population of bristle-thighed curlews numbers less than 10,000 individuals, ability to sense these patterns is crucial.

The champion long-distance, non-stop migrant is the bar-tailed godwit. This large, orangish shorebird with a distinctly upturned bill breeds across western and northern Alaska. Like Pacific golden-plovers, bar-tailed godwits

congregate during the fall in tidal lagoons of Bristol Bay to pack on fat reserves. When these reserves are stockpiled and winds are favorable, the godwits take off and do not land until they reach New Zealand, 6,500 miles away. This may be the longest non-stop migration of any bird. What makes this feat even more spectacular is the realization that young godwits born in the past summer undertake this journey with no assistance from their parents. Godwits, along with other migrant birds, likely use several tools to navigate across unfamiliar terrain. Research indicates that birds use stars and the sun as compasses and can use the earth's magnetic fields to decide which direction to fly. Many of

Homer school children learn about birds through U.S. Fish and Wildlife Service's Shorebird Sister Schools Program, a cooperative effort among communities to foster habitat conservation and knowledge of migratory birds. (Kevin Hartwell)

Waiting to be fed, fox sparrow chicks stretch their beaks wide. Songbird parents feed their nestlings feverishly in the mornings, taking a break to feed themselves only after the young are satiated. (George Wuerthner)

A mosquito perches on a nesting short-eared owl's beak. The nest, a sparsely lined shallow depression on the ground in an open meadow or near a marsh, is typical habitat for the mosquito, an insect many Alaskans refer to jokingly as "Alaska's state bird." (Don Cornelius)

these navigation skills are innate.

En route, bar-tailed godwits may pass flocks of sooty shearwaters heading north. Shearwaters are burrow-nesting seabirds that spend most of their life on the ocean. In direct contrast to the southward-migrating godwit, the shearwater has concluded its breeding season in New Zealand and is heading north to feed in the rich waters of Alaska during its winter. Unlike godwits, shearwaters have the ability to land and rest on the ocean.

Because many of Alaska's breeding birds travel long distances during migration, they are subject to a variety of perils, from loss of habitat to vagaries of weather. Conservation of migratory birds clearly requires cooperation across state, international, and hemispheric boundaries. Only then will people be able to enjoy the wonderful return of migratory birds to Alaska each spring. The fact that some species of Alaska-breeding bird can be found on every continent during the northern winter makes this task daunting.

Nonetheless, governmental and non-governmental agencies need to build strong partnerships for the conservation of migratory birds. Citizens can help too. Activities span the entire range of Alaska's breeding birds, and many organizations throughout the Americas and Asia are furthering migratory and resident bird conservation. •

Checklist of Alaska Birds, 9th edition — 1999

As of 1 January 1999 the list of avian taxa known in Alaska included 456 naturally occurring species in 59 families and 19 orders. This checklist is based primarily on archived specimens, but includes a few species known only from (archived) photos or audio recordings. An appended "unsubstantiated list" comprises an additional 29 species attributed to Alaska on the basis of observation alone. Phylogenetic sequence, limits of orders and families, and scientific and English names follow *The A.O.U. Check-list of North American Birds* (Seventh ed., 1998).

✓ Rare (Annual or probably annual in small numbers; most such species occur at the perimeter of Alaska, in season; a few are scarce residents)

★ Casual (Not annual; these species are beyond the periphery of annual range, but recur in Alaska at irregular intervals, usually in seasonal and regional patterns)

☆ Accidental (one or two Alaska records)

Order GAVIIFORMES, Family GAVIIDAE
__ Red-throated Loon *Gavia stellata*
__ Arctic Loon *Gavia arctica* ✓
__ Pacific Loon *Gavia pacifica*
__ Common Loon *Gavia immer*
__ Yellow-billed Loon *Gavia adamsii*

Order PODICIPEDIFORMES, Family PODICIPEDIDAE
__ Pied-billed Grebe *Podilymbus podiceps* ✓
__ Horned Grebe *Podiceps auritus*
__ Red-necked Grebe *Podiceps grisegena*
__ Eared Grebe *Podiceps nigricollis* ☆
__ Western Grebe *Aechmophorus occidentalis*

Order PROCELLARIIFORMES, Family DIOMEDEIDAE
__ Laysan Albatross *Phoebastria immutabilis*
__ Black-footed Albatross *Phoebastria nigripes*
__ Short-tailed Albatross *Phoebastria albatrus* ✓

Family PROCELLARIIDAE
__ Northern Fulmar *Fulmarus glacialis*
__ Mottled Petrel *Pterodroma inexpectata*
__ Cook's Petrel *Pterodroma cookii* ☆
__ Buller's Shearwater *Puffinus bulleri* ✓
__ Sooty Shearwater *Puffinus griseus*
__ Short-tailed Shearwater *Puffinus tenuirostris*

Family HYDROBATIDAE
__ Fork-tailed Storm-Petrel *Oceanodroma furcata*
__ Leach's Storm-Petrel *Oceanodroma leucorhoa*

Order PELECANIFORMES, Family PELECANIDAE
__ American White Pelican *Pelecanus erythrorhynchos* ☆

Family PHALACROCORACIDAE
__ Brandt's Cormorant *Phalacrocorax penicillatus* ✓
__ Double-crested Cormorant *Phalacrocorax auritus*
__ Red-faced Cormorant *Phalacrocorax urile*
__ Pelagic Cormorant *Phalacrocorax pelagicus*

Family FREGATIDAE
__ Magnificent Frigatebird *Fregata magnificens* ☆

Order CICONIIFORMES, Family ARDEIDAE
__ American Bittern *Botaurus lentiginosus* ✓
__ Yellow Bittern *Ixobrychus sinensis* ☆
__ Great Blue Heron *Ardea herodias*
__ Great Egret *Ardea alba* ★
__ Chinese Egret *Egretta eulophotes* ☆
__ Chinese Pond Heron *Ardeola bacchus* ☆
__ Cattle Egret *Bubulcus ibis* ★
__ Green Heron *Butorides virescens* ☆
__ Black-crowned Night-Heron *Nycticorax nycticorax* ★

Family CATHARTIDAE
__ Turkey Vulture *Cathartes aura* ★

Order ANSERIFORMES, Family ANATIDAE
__ Bean Goose Anser *fabalis* ★
__ Greater White-fronted Goose *Anser albifrons*
__ Lesser White-fronted Goose *Anser erythropus* ☆
__ Emperor Goose *Chen canagica*
__ Snow Goose *Chen caerulescens*
__ Ross's Goose *Chen rossii* ★
__ Canada Goose *Branta canadensis*
__ Brant *Branta bernicla*
__ Trumpeter Swan *Cygnus buccinator*
__ Tundra Swan *Cygnus columbianus*
__ Whooper Swan *Cygnus cygnus* ✓
__ Wood Duck *Aix sponsa* ★
__ Gadwall *Anas strepera*
__ Falcated Duck *Anas falcata* ★
__ Eurasian Wigeon *Anas penelope*
__ American Wigeon *Anas americana*
__ American Black Duck *Anas rubripes* ☆
__ Mallard *Anas platyrhynchos*
__ Spot-billed Duck *Anas poecilorhyncha* ★
__ Blue-winged Teal *Anas discors*
__ Cinnamon Teal *Anas cyanoptera* ✓
__ Northern Shoveler *Anas clypeata*
__ Northern Pintail *Anas acuta*
__ Garganey *Anas querquedula* ✓
__ Baikal Teal *Anas formosa* ★
__ Green-winged Teal *Anas crecca*
__ Canvasback *Aythya valisineria*
__ Redhead *Aythya americana*
__ Common Pochard *Aythya ferina* ✓
__ Ring-necked Duck *Aythya collaris*
__ Tufted Duck *Aythya fuligula* ✓
__ Greater Scaup *Aythya marila*
__ Lesser Scaup *Aythya affinis*
__ Steller's Eider *Polysticta stelleri*
__ Spectacled Eider *Somateria fischeri*
__ King Eider *Somateria spectabilis*
__ Common Eider *Somateria mollissima*
__ Harlequin Duck *Histrionicus histrionicus*
__ Surf Scoter *Melanitta perspicillata*
__ White-winged Scoter *Melanitta fusca*
__ Black Scoter *Melanitta nigra*
__ Oldsquaw *Clangula hyemalis*
__ Bufflehead *Bucephala albeola*
__ Common Goldeneye *Bucephala clangula*
__ Barrow's Goldeneye *Bucephala islandica*
__ Smew *Mergellus albellus* ✓
__ Hooded Merganser *Lophodytes cucullatus*
__ Common Merganser *Mergus merganser*
__ Red-breasted Merganser *Mergus serrator*
__ Ruddy Duck *Oxyura jamaicensis* ★

Order FALCONIFORMES, Family ACCIPITRIDAE
__ Osprey *Pandion haliaetus*
__ Bald Eagle *Haliaeetus leucocephalus*
__ White-tailed Eagle *Haliaeetus albicilla* ★
__ Steller's Sea-Eagle *Haliaeetus pelagicus* ★
__ Northern Harrier *Circus cyaneus*
__ Sharp-shinned Hawk *Accipiter striatus*
__ Northern Goshawk *Accipiter gentilis*
__ Swainson's Hawk *Buteo swainsoni* ✓
__ Red-tailed Hawk *Buteo jamaicensis*
__ Rough-legged Hawk *Buteo lagopus*
__ Golden Eagle *Aquila chrysaetos*

Family FALCONIDAE
__ Eurasian Kestrel *Falco tinnunculus* ★
__ American Kestrel *Falco sparverius*
__ Merlin *Falco columbarius*
__ Eurasian Hobby *Falco subbuteo* ★
__ Gyrfalcon *Falco rusticolus*
__ Peregrine Falcon *Falco peregrinus*

Order GALLIFORMES, Family PHASIANIDAE

__ Ruffed Grouse *Bonasa umbellus*
__ Spruce Grouse *Falcipennis canadensis*
__ Willow Ptarmigan *Lagopus lagopus*
__ Rock Ptarmigan *Lagopus mutus*
__ White-tailed Ptarmigan *Lagopus leucurus*
__ Blue Grouse *Dendragapus obscurus*
__ Sharp-tailed Grouse *Tympanuchus phasianellus*

Order GRUIFORMES, Family RALLIDAE

__ Virginia Rail *Rallus limicola* ★
__ Sora *Porzana carolina* ✓
__ Eurasian Coot *Fulica atra* ☆
__ American Coot *Fulica americana* ✓

Family GRUIDAE

__ Sandhill Crane *Grus canadensis*
__ Common Crane *Grus grus* ☆

Order CHARADRIIFORMES, Family CHARADRIIDAE

__ Black-bellied Plover *Pluvialis squatarola*
__ American Golden-Plover *Pluvialis dominica*
__ Pacific Golden-Plover *Pluvialis fulva*
__ Mongolian Plover *Charadrius mongolus* ✓
__ Snowy Plover *Charadrius alexandrinus* ☆
__ Common Ringed Plover *Charadrius hiaticula* ✓
__ Semipalmated Plover *Charadrius semipalmatus*
__ Little Ringed Plover *Charadrius dubius* ★
__ Killdeer *Charadrius vociferus*
__ Eurasian Dotterel *Charadrius morinellus* ✓

Family HAEMATOPODIDAE

__ Black Oystercatcher *Haematopus bachmani*

Family RECURVIROSTRIDAE

__ Black-winged Stilt *Himantopus himantopus* ☆
__ American Avocet *Recurvirostra americana* ☆

Family SCOLOPACIDAE

__ Common Greenshank *Tringa nebularia* ✓
__ Greater Yellowlegs *Tringa melanoleuca*
__ Lesser Yellowlegs *Tringa flavipes*
__ Marsh Sandpiper *Tringa stagnatilis* ☆
__ Spotted Redshank *Tringa erythropus* ✓
__ Wood Sandpiper *Tringa glareola* ✓
__ Green Sandpiper *Tringa ochropus* ★
__ Solitary Sandpiper *Tringa solitaria*
__ Wandering Tattler *Heteroscelus incanus*
__ Gray-tailed Tattler *Heteroscelus brevipes*
__ Common Sandpiper *Actitis hypoleucos* ✓
__ Spotted Sandpiper *Actitis macularia*
__ Terek Sandpiper *Xenus cinereus* ✓
__ Upland Sandpiper *Bartramia longicauda*
__ Little Curlew *Numenius minutus* ☆
__ Eskimo Curlew *Numenius borealis* ☆ not since 1886
__ Whimbrel *Numenius phaeopus*
__ Bristle-thighed Curlew *Numenius tahitiensis*
__ Far Eastern Curlew *Numenius madagascariensis* ★
__ Black-tailed Godwit *Limosa limosa* ★
__ Hudsonian Godwit *Limosa haemastica*
__ Bar-tailed Godwit *Limosa lapponica*
__ Marbled Godwit *Limosa fedoa* ✓
__ Ruddy Turnstone *Arenaria interpres*
__ Black Turnstone *Arenaria melanocephala*
__ Surfbird *Aphriza virgata*
__ Great Knot *Calidris tenuirostris* ★
__ Red Knot *Calidris canutus*
__ Sanderling *Calidris alba*
__ Semipalmated Sandpiper *Calidris pusilla*
__ Western Sandpiper *Calidris mauri*
__ Red-necked Stint *Calidris ruficollis* ✓
__ Little Stint *Calidris minuta* ★
__ Temminck's Stint *Calidris temminckii* ★
__ Long-toed Stint *Calidris subminuta* ✓
__ Least Sandpiper *Calidris minutilla*
__ White-rumped Sandpiper *Calidris fuscicollis* ✓
__ Baird's Sandpiper *Calidris bairdii*
__ Pectoral Sandpiper *Calidris melanotos*
__ Sharp-tailed Sandpiper *Calidris acuminata*
__ Purple Sandpiper *Calidris maritima* ☆
__ Rock Sandpiper *Calidris ptilocnemis*
__ Dunlin *Calidris alpina*
__ Curlew Sandpiper *Calidris ferruginea* ★
__ Stilt Sandpiper *Calidris himantopus*
__ Spoonbill Sandpiper *Eurynorhynchus pygmeus* ★
__ Broad-billed Sandpiper *Limicola falcinellus* ★
__ Buff-breasted Sandpiper *Tryngites subruficollis*
__ Ruff *Philomachus pugnax* ✓
__ Short-billed Dowitcher *Limnodromus griseus*
__ Long-billed Dowitcher *Limnodromus scolopaceus*
__ Jack Snipe *Lymnocryptes minimus* ☆
__ Common Snipe *Gallinago gallinago*
__ Pin-tailed Snipe *Gallinago stenura* ☆
__ Wilson's Phalarope *Phalaropus tricolor* ★
__ Red-necked Phalarope *Phalaropus lobatus*
__ Red Phalarope *Phalaropus fulicaria*

Family GLAREOLIDAE

__ Oriental Pratincole *Glareola maldivarum* ☆

Family LARIDAE

__ South Polar Skua *Catharacta maccormicki* ★
__ Pomarine Jaeger *Stercorarius pomarinus*
__ Parasitic Jaeger *Stercorarius parasiticus*
__ Long-tailed Jaeger *Stercorarius longicaudus*
__ Franklin's Gull *Larus pipixcan* ★
__ Black-headed Gull *Larus ridibundus* ✓
__ Bonaparte's Gull *Larus philadelphia*
__ Heermann's Gull *Larus heermanni* ★
__ Black-tailed Gull *Larus crassirostris* ★
__ Mew Gull *Larus canus*
__ Ring-billed Gull *Larus delawarensis* ✓
__ California Gull *Larus californicus*
__ Herring Gull *Larus argentatus*
__ Iceland Gull *Larus glaucoides* (including thayeri)
__ Lesser Black-backed Gull *Larus fuscus* ★
__ Slaty-backed Gull *Larus schistisagus*
__ Western Gull *Larus occidentalis* ★
__ Glaucous-winged Gull *Larus glaucescens*
__ Glaucous Gull *Larus hyperboreus*
__ Great Black-backed Gull *Larus marinus* ☆
__ Sabine's Gull *Xema sabini*
__ Black-legged Kittiwake *Rissa tridactyla*
__ Red-legged Kittiwake *Rissa brevirostris*
__ Ross's Gull *Rhodostethia rosea*
__ Ivory Gull *Pagophila eburnea*
__ Caspian Tern *Sterna caspia* ✓
__ Common Tern *Sterna hirundo* ✓
__ Arctic Tern *Sterna paradisaea*
__ Forster's Tern *Sterna forsteri* ☆
__ Aleutian Tern *Sterna aleutica*
__ Sooty Tern *Sterna fuscata* ☆
__ White-winged Tern *Chlidonias leucopterus* ★
__ Black Tern *Chlidonias niger* ★

Family ALCIDAE

__ Dovekie *Alle alle* ✓
__ Common Murre *Uria aalge*
__ Thick-billed Murre *Uria lomvia*
__ Black Guillemot *Cepphus grylle*
__ Pigeon Guillemot *Cepphus columba*
__ Long-billed Murrelet *Brachyramphus perdix* ☆
__ Marbled Murrelet *Brachyramphus marmoratus*
__ Kittlitz's Murrelet *Brachyramphus brevirostris*
__ Ancient Murrelet *Synthliboramphus antiquus*
__ Cassin's Auklet *Ptychoramphus aleuticus*
__ Parakeet Auklet *Aethia psittacula*
__ Least Auklet *Aethia pusilla*
__ Whiskered Auklet *Aethia pygmaea*
__ Crested Auklet *Aethia cristatella*
__ Rhinoceros Auklet *Cerorhinca monocerata*
__ Horned Puffin *Fratercula corniculata*
__ Tufted Puffin *Fratercula cirrhata*

Order COLUMBIFORMES, Family COLUMBIDAE

__ Band-tailed Pigeon *Columba fasciata* ✓
__ Oriental Turtle-Dove *Streptopelia orientalis* ★
__ White-winged Dove *Zenaida asiatica* ☆
__ Mourning Dove *Zenaida macroura* ✓

Order CUCULIFORMES,
Family CUCULIDAE
__ Common Cuckoo *Cuculus canorus* ★
__ Oriental Cuckoo *Cuculus saturatus* ★
__ Yellow-billed Cuckoo *Coccyzus americanus* ★

Order STRIGIFORMES,
Family STRIGIDAE
__ Oriental Scops-Owl *Otus sunia* ☆
__ Western Screech-Owl *Otus kennicottii* ✓
__ Great Horned Owl *Bubo virginianus*
__ Snowy Owl *Nyctea scandiaca*
__ Northern Hawk Owl *Surnia ulula*
__ Northern Pygmy-Owl *Glaucidium gnoma* ✓
__ Barred Owl *Strix varia* ✓
__ Great Gray Owl *Strix nebulosa*
__ Long-eared Owl *Asio otus* ★
__ Short-eared Owl *Asio flammeus*
__ Boreal Owl *Aegolius funereus*
__ Northern Saw-whet Owl *Aegolius acadicus*

Order CAPRIMULGIFORMES,
Family CAPRIMULGIDAE
__ Lesser Nighthawk *Chordeiles acutipennis* ☆
__ Common Nighthawk *Chordeiles minor* ✓
__ Whip-poor-will *Caprimulgus vociferus* ☆
__ Jungle Nightjar *Caprimulgus indicus* ☆

Order APODIFORMES,
Family APODIDAE
__ Black Swift *Cypseloides niger*
__ Chimney Swift *Chaetura pelagica* ☆
__ Vaux's Swift *Chaetura vauxi*
__ White-throated Needletail *Hirundapus caudacutus* ★
__ Common Swift *Apus apus* ☆
__ Fork-tailed Swift *Apus pacificus* ★

Family TROCHILIDAE
__ Ruby-throated Hummingbird *Archilochus colubris* ☆
__ Anna's Hummingbird *Calypte anna* ✓
__ Costa's Hummingbird *Calypte costae* ★
__ Rufous Hummingbird *Selasphorus rufus*

Order UPUPIFORMES,
Family UPUPIDAE
__ Eurasian Hoopoe *Upupa epops* ☆

Order CORACIIFORMES,
Family ALCEDINIDAE
__ Belted Kingfisher *Ceryle alcyon*

Order PICIFORMES,
Family PICIDAE
__ Eurasian Wryneck *Jynx torquilla* ☆
__ Yellow-bellied Sapsucker *Sphyrapicus varius* ✓
__ Red-breasted Sapsucker *Sphyrapicus ruber*
__ Great Spotted Woodpecker *Dendrocopos major* ✓
__ Downy Woodpecker *Picoides pubescens*
__ Hairy Woodpecker *Picoides villosus*
__ Three-toed Woodpecker *Picoides tridactylus*
__ Black-backed Woodpecker *Picoides arcticus*
__ Northern Flicker *Colaptes auratus*

Order PASSERIFORMES,
Family TYRANNIDAE
__ Olive-sided Flycatcher *Contopus cooperi*
__ Western Wood-Pewee *Contopus sordidulus*
__ Yellow-bellied Flycatcher *Empidonax flaviventris* ✓
__ Alder Flycatcher *Empidonax alnorum*
__ Willow Flycatcher *Empidonax traillii* ★
__ Least Flycatcher *Empidonax minimus* ✓
__ Hammond's Flycatcher *Empidonax hammondii*
__ Dusky Flycatcher *Empidonax oberholseri* ★
__ Pacific-slope Flycatcher *Empidonax difficilis*
__ Eastern Phoebe *Sayornis phoebe* ★
__ Say's Phoebe *Sayornis saya*
__ Great Crested Flycatcher *Myiarchus crinitus* ☆
__ Tropical Kingbird *Tyrannus melancholicus* ★
__ Western Kingbird *Tyrannus verticalis* ★
__ Eastern Kingbird *Tyrannus tyrannus* ✓

Family LANIIDAE
__ Brown Shrike *Lanius cristatus* ★
__ Northern Shrike *Lanius excubitor*

Family VIREONIDAE
__ Cassin's Vireo *Vireo cassinii* ★
__ Warbling Vireo *Vireo gilvus*
__ Philadelphia Vireo *Vireo philadelphicus* ★
__ Red-eyed Vireo *Vireo olivaceus* ✓

Family CORVIDAE
__ Gray Jay *Perisoreus canadensis*
__ Steller's Jay *Cyanocitta stelleri*
__ Clark's Nutcracker *Nucifraga columbiana* ★
__ Black-billed Magpie *Pica pica*
__ American Crow *Corvus brachyrhynchos* ✓
__ Northwestern Crow *Corvus caurinus*
__ Common Raven *Corvus corax*

Family ALAUDIDAE
__ Sky Lark *Alauda arvensis* ✓
__ Horned Lark *Eremophila alpestris*

Family HIRUNDINIDAE
__ Purple Martin *Progne subis* ★
__ Tree Swallow *Tachycineta bicolor*
__ Violet-green Swallow *Tachycineta thalassina*
__ Northern Rough-winged Swallow *Stelgidopteryx serripennis* ✓
__ Bank Swallow *Riparia riparia*
__ Cliff Swallow *Petrochelidon pyrrhonota*
__ Barn Swallow *Hirundo rustica*
__ Common House-Martin *Delichon urbica* ★

Family PARIDAE
__ Black-capped Chickadee *Poecile atricapillus*
__ Mountain Chickadee *Poecile gambeli* ★
__ Chestnut-backed Chickadee *Poecile rufescens*
__ Boreal Chickadee *Poecile hudsonicus*
__ Gray-headed Chickadee *Poecile cinctus* ✓

Family SITTIDAE
__ Red-breasted Nuthatch *Sitta canadensis*

Family CERTHIIDAE
__ Brown Creeper *Certhia americana*

Family TROGLODYTIDAE
__ Winter Wren *Troglodytes troglodytes*

Family CINCLIDAE
__ American Dipper *Cinclus mexicanus*

Family REGULIDAE
__ Golden-crowned Kinglet *Regulus satrapa*
__ Ruby-crowned Kinglet *Regulus calendula*

Family SYLVIIDAE
__ Middendorff's Grasshopper-Warbler *Locustella ochotensis* ★
__ Lanceolated Warbler *Locustella lanceolata* ☆
__ Wood Warbler *Phylloscopus sibilatrix* ☆
__ Dusky Warbler *Phylloscopus fuscatus* ★
__ Arctic Warbler *Phylloscopus borealis*

Family MUSCICAPIDAE
__ Narcissus Flycatcher *Ficedula narcissina* ☆
__ Red-breasted Flycatcher *Ficedula parva* ★
__ Siberian Flycatcher *Muscicapa sibirica* ★
__ Gray-spotted Flycatcher *Muscicapa griseisticta* ★
__ Asian Brown Flycatcher *Muscicapa dauurica* ☆

Family TURDIDAE
__ Siberian Rubythroat *Luscinia calliope* ✓
__ Bluethroat *Luscinia svecica*
__ Siberian Blue Robin *Luscinia cyane* ☆
__ Red-flanked Bluetail *Tarsiger cyanurus* ★
__ Northern Wheatear *Oenanthe oenanthe*
__ Stonechat *Saxicola torquatus* ★
__ Mountain Bluebird *Sialia currucoides* ✓
__ Townsend's Solitaire *Myadestes townsendi*
__ Veery *Catharus fuscescens* ★
__ Gray-cheeked Thrush *Catharus minimus*
__ Swainson's Thrush *Catharus ustulatus*
__ Hermit Thrush *Catharus guttatus*
__ Eyebrowed Thrush *Turdus obscurus* ✓
__ Dusky Thrush *Turdus naumanni* ★

__ Fieldfare *Turdus pilaris* ★
__ American Robin *Turdus migratorius*
__ Varied Thrush *Ixoreus naevius*

Family MIMIDAE
__ Gray Catbird *Dumetella carolinensis* ☆
__ Northern Mockingbird *Mimus polyglottos* ★
__ Brown Thrasher *Toxostoma rufum* ★

Family STURNIDAE
__ European Starling *Sturnus vulgaris*

Family PRUNELLIDAE
__ Siberian Accentor *Prunella montanella* ★

Family MOTACILLIDAE
__ Yellow Wagtail *Motacilla flava*
__ Gray Wagtail *Motacilla cinerea* ★
__ White Wagtail *Motacilla alba* ✓
__ Black-backed Wagtail *Motacilla lugens* ✓
__ Tree Pipit *Anthus trivialis* ☆
__ Olive-backed Pipit *Anthus hodgsoni* ★
__ Pechora Pipit *Anthus gustavi* ★
__ Red-throated Pipit *Anthus cervinus*
__ American Pipit *Anthus rubescens*

Family BOMBYCILLIDAE
__ Bohemian Waxwing *Bombycilla garrulus*
__ Cedar Waxwing *Bombycilla cedrorum*

Family PARULIDAE
__ Tennessee Warbler *Vermivora peregrina* ✓
__ Orange-crowned Warbler *Vermivora celata*
__ Yellow Warbler *Dendroica petechia*
__ Chestnut-sided Warbler *Dendroica pensylvanica* ☆
__ Magnolia Warbler *Dendroica magnolia* ✓
__ Cape May Warbler *Dendroica tigrina* ★
__ Yellow-rumped Warbler *Dendroica coronata*
__ Black-throated Green Warbler *Dendroica virens* ☆
__ Townsend's Warbler *Dendroica townsendi*
__ Prairie Warbler *Dendroica discolor* ☆
__ Palm Warbler *Dendroica palmarum* ★

__ Blackpoll Warbler *Dendroica striata*
__ Black-and-white Warbler *Mniotilta varia* ★
__ American Redstart *Setophaga ruticilla*
__ Ovenbird *Seiurus aurocapillus* ★
__ Northern Waterthrush *Seiurus noveboracensis*
__ Mourning Warbler *Oporornis philadelphia* ☆
__ MacGillivray's Warbler *Oporornis tolmiei*
__ Common Yellowthroat *Geothlypis trichas*
__ Wilson's Warbler *Wilsonia pusilla*
__ Canada Warbler *Wilsonia canadensis* ☆

Family THRAUPIDAE
__ Scarlet Tanager *Piranga olivacea* ☆
__ Western Tanager *Piranga ludoviciana*

Family EMBERIZIDAE
__ Spotted Towhee *Pipilo maculatus* ★
__ American Tree Sparrow *Spizella arborea*
__ Chipping Sparrow *Spizela passerina*
__ Clay-colored Sparrow *Spizella pallida* ★
__ Brewer's Sparrow *Spizella breweri* ✓
__ Lark Sparrow *Chondestes grammacus* ☆
__ Savannah Sparrow *Passerculus sandwichensis*
__ Fox Sparrow *Passerella iliaca*
__ Song Sparrow *Melospiza melodia*
__ Lincoln's Sparrow *Melospiza lincolnii*
__ Swamp Sparrow *Melospiza georgiana* ★
__ White-throated Sparrow *Zonotrichia albicollis* ★
__ Harris's Sparrow *Zonotrichia querula* ★
__ White-crowned Sparrow *Zonotrichia leucophrys*
__ Golden-crowned Sparrow *Zonotrichia atricapilla*
__ Dark-eyed Junco *Junco hyemalis*
__ Lapland Longspur *Calcarius lapponicus*
__ Smith's Longspur *Calcarius pictus*
__ Pine Bunting *Emberiza leucocephalos* ☆
__ Little Bunting *Emberiza pusilla* ★
__ Rustic Bunting *Emberiza rustica* ✓
__ Yellow-throated Bunting *Emberiza elegans* ☆
__ Yellow-breasted Bunting *Emberiza aureola* ★
__ Gray Bunting *Emberiza variabilis* ☆

__ Pallas's Bunting *Emberiza pallasi* ★
__ Reed Bunting *Emberiza schoeniclus* ★
__ Snow Bunting *Plectrophenax nivalis*
__ McKay's Bunting *Plectrophenax hyperboreus*

Family CARDINALIDAE
__ Rose-breasted Grosbeak *Pheucticus ludovicianus* ★
__ Black-headed Grosbeak *Pheucticus melanocephalus* ★
__ Blue Grosbeak *Guiraca caerulea* ☆
__ Indigo Bunting *Passerina cyanea* ★

Family ICTERIDAE
__ Bobolink *Dolichonyx oryzivorus* ☆
__ Red-winged Blackbird *Agelaius phoeniceus*
__ Western Meadowlark *Sturnella neglecta* ★
__ Yellow-headed Blackbird *Xanthocephalus xanthocephalus* ★
__ Rusty Blackbird *Euphagus carolinus*
__ Brewer's Blackbird *Euphagus cyanocephalus* ★
__ Common Grackle *Quiscalus quiscula* ★
__ Brown-headed Cowbird *Molothrus ater* ✓

Family FRINGILLIDAE
__ Brambling *Fringilla montifringilla* ✓
__ Gray-crowned Rosy-Finch *Leucosticte tephrocotis*
__ Pine Grosbeak *Pinicola enucleator*
__ Common Rosefinch *Carpodacus erythrinus* ★
__ Purple Finch *Carpodacus purpureus* ★
__ Cassin's Finch *Carpodacus cassinii* ★
__ House Finch *Carpodacus mexicanus* ★
__ Red Crossbill *Loxia curvirostra*
__ White-winged Crossbill *Loxia leucoptera*
__ Common Redpoll *Carduelis flammea*
__ Hoary Redpoll *Carduelis hornemanni*
__ Eurasian Siskin *Carduelis spinus* ☆
__ Pine Siskin *Carduelis pinus*
__ American Goldfinch *Carduelis tristis* ☆
__ Oriental Greenfinch *Carduelis sinica* ★
__ Eurasian Bullfinch *Pyrrhula pyrrhula* ★

__ Evening Grosbeak *Coccothraustes vespertinus* ★
__ Hawfinch *Coccothraustes coccothraustes* ★

Family PASSERIDAE
__ House Sparrow *Passer domesticus* ★

Unsubstantiated in Alaska

Clark's Grebe *Aechmophorus clarkii*
Pink-footed Shearwater *Puffinus creatopus*
Flesh-footed Shearwater *Puffinus carneipes*
Manx Shearwater *Puffinus puffinus*
Little Shearwater *Puffinus assimilis*
Snowy Egret *Egretta thula*
Gray Frog-Hawk *Accipiter soloensis*
Cooper's Hawk *Accipiter cooperii*
Common Buzzard *Buteo buteo*
Yellow Rail *Coturnicops noveboracensis*
European Golden-plover *Pluvialis apricaria*
Willet *Catoptrophorus semipalmatus*
Long-billed Curlew *Numenius americanus*
Laughing Gull *Larus atricilla*
Little Gull *Larus minutus*
Calliope Hummingbird *Stellula calliope*
Pileated Woodpecker *Dryocopus pileatus*
Scissor-tailed Flycatcher *Tyrannus forficatus*
Great Tit *Parus major*
Mugimaki Flycatcher *Ficedula mugimaki*
Nashville Warbler *Vermivora ruficapilla*
Northern Parula *Parula americana*
Black-throated Gray Warbler *Dendroica nigrescens*
Hermit Warbler *Dendroica occidentalis*
Bay-breasted Warbler *Dendroica castanea*
Kentucky Warbler *Oporornis formosus*
Chestnut-collared Longspur *Calcarius ornatus*
Lazuli Bunting *Passerina amoena*
Bullock's Oriole *Icterus bullockii*

Compiled and © 1999 by Daniel D. Gibson, University of Alaska Museum, Fairbanks, Alaska 99775-6960.

Bibliography

Anderson, Cary. *Alaska's Magnificent Eagles*, Alaska Geographic, vol. 24, no. 4. Edited by Penny Rennick. Anchorage: Alaska Geographic Society, 1997.

Armstrong, Robert H. *Guide to the Birds of Alaska*. 4th ed. Anchorage: Alaska Northwest Books, 1995.

Bird, David M., PhD. *The Bird Almanac: The Ultimate Guide to Essential Facts and Figures of the World's Birds*. Buffalo: Firefly, 1999.

Gabrielson, Ira N. and Frederick C. Lincoln. *The Birds of Alaska*. Harrisburg: The Stackpole Co. and Washington, D.C.: Wildlife Management Institute, 1959.

Gruson, Edward S. *Words for Birds: A Lexicon of North American Birds with Biographical Notes*. New York: Quadrangle, 1972.

Kessel, Brina and Daniel D. Gibson. *Status and distribution of Alaska birds*. N.p. [California]: Cooper Ornithological Society, 1978.

Mearns, Barbara and Richard. *Audubon to Xantus: The Lives of Those Commemorated in North American Bird Names*. London: Academic Press, 1992.

Murie, Adolph. *Birds of Mount McKinley National Park Alaska*. Mount McKinley Natural History Association, 1963.

Terres, John K. *The Audubon Society Encyclopedia of North American Birds*. New York: Alfred A. Knopf, 1980.

http://homeralaska.org/shorebird.htm (Kachemak Bay Shorebird Festival)
www.alaskabird.org (Alaska Bird Observatory, Fairbanks)
www.birdtlc.org (Bird Treatment and Learning Center, Anchorage)
www.alaskaraptor.org (Alaska Raptor Center, Sitka)
www.americanbirding.org/ (American Birding Association)
www.audubon.org/chapter/ak/ak (National Audubon Society, State Office)
www.cooper.org/ (Cooper Ornithological Society)
www.fws.gov/index.html (U.S. Fish and Wildlife Service)
www.nmnh.si.edu/vert/birds/birds.html (Division of Birds, National Museum of Natural History, Smithsonian Institution)
http://pica.wru.umt.edu/AOU/AOU.html (The American Ornithologists' Union)
www.uaf.edu/museum (University of Alaska Fairbanks Museum)

Index

PHOTOGRAPHERS

ALASKA GEOGRAPHIC® Back Issues

The North Slope, Vol. 1, No. 1. Out of print.
One Man's Wilderness, Vol. 1, No. 2. Out of print.
Admiralty...Island in Contention, Vol. 1, No. 3. $9.95.
Fisheries of the North Pacific, Vol. 1, No. 4. Out of print.
Alaska-Yukon Wild Flowers, Vol. 2, No. 1. Out of print.
Richard Harrington's Yukon, Vol. 2, No. 2. Out of print.
Prince William Sound, Vol. 2, No. 3. Out of print.
Yakutat: The Turbulent Crescent, Vol. 2, No. 4. Out of print.
Glacier Bay: Old Ice, New Land, Vol. 3, No. 1. Out of print.
The Land: Eye of the Storm, Vol. 3, No. 2. Out of print.
Richard Harrington's Antarctic, Vol. 3, No. 3. $9.95.
The Silver Years, Vol. 3, No. 4. $19.95.
Alaska's Volcanoes, Vol. 4, No. 1. Out of print.
The Brooks Range, Vol. 4, No. 2. Out of print.
Kodiak: Island of Change, Vol. 4, No. 3. Out of print.
Wilderness Proposals, Vol. 4, No. 4. Out of print.
Cook Inlet Country, Vol. 5, No. 1. Out of print.
Southeast: Alaska's Panhandle, Vol. 5, No. 2. Out of print.
Bristol Bay Basin, Vol. 5, No. 3. Out of print.
Alaska Whales and Whaling, Vol. 5, No. 4. $19.95.
Yukon-Kuskokwim Delta, Vol. 6, No. 1. Out of print.
Aurora Borealis, Vol. 6, No. 2. $19.95.
Alaska's Native People, Vol. 6, No. 3. $29.95. Limited.
The Stikine River, Vol. 6, No. 4. $9.95.
Alaska's Great Interior, Vol. 7, No. 1. $19.95.
Photographic Geography of Alaska, Vol. 7, No. 2. Out of print.
The Aleutians, Vol. 7, No. 3. Out of print.
Klondike Lost, Vol. 7, No. 4. Out of print.
Wrangell-Saint Elias, Vol. 8, No. 1. $21.95. Out of print.
Alaska Mammals, Vol. 8, No. 2. Out of print.
The Kotzebue Basin, Vol. 8, No. 3. Out of print.
Alaska National Interest Lands, Vol. 8, No. 4. $19.95.
* Alaska's Glaciers, Vol. 9, No. 1. Rev. 1993. $21.95. Limited.
Sitka and Its Ocean/Island World, Vol. 9, No. 2. Out of print.
Islands of the Seals: The Pribilofs, Vol. 9, No. 3. $9.95.
Alaska's Oil/Gas & Minerals Industry, Vol. 9, No. 4. $9.95.
Adventure Roads North, Vol. 10, No. 1. $9.95.
Anchorage and the Cook Inlet Basin, Vol. 10, No. 2. $19.95.
Alaska's Salmon Fisheries, Vol. 10, No. 3. $9.95.
Up the Koyukuk, Vol. 10, No. 4. $9.95.
Nome: City of the Golden Beaches, Vol. 11, No. 1. $19.95.
Alaska's Farms and Gardens, Vol. 11, No. 2. $19.95.
Chilkat River Valley, Vol. 11, No. 3. $9.95.
Alaska Steam, Vol. 11, No. 4. $19.95.
Northwest Territories, Vol. 12, No. 1. $9.95.

Alaska's Forest Resources, Vol. 12, No. 2. $9.95.
Alaska Native Arts and Crafts, Vol. 12, No. 3. $24.95.
Our Arctic Year, Vol. 12, No. 4. $19.95.
* Where Mountains Meet the Sea, Vol. 13, No. 1. $19.95.
Backcountry Alaska, Vol. 13, No. 2. $9.95.
British Columbia's Coast, Vol. 13, No. 3. $9.95.
Lake Clark/Lake Iliamna, Vol. 13, No. 4. Out of print.
Dogs of the North, Vol. 14, No. 1. Out of print.
South/Southeast Alaska, Vol. 14, No. 2. $21.95. Limited.
Alaska's Seward Peninsula, Vol. 14, No. 3. $19.95.
The Upper Yukon Basin, Vol. 14, No. 4. $19.95.
Glacier Bay: Icy Wilderness, Vol. 15, No. 1. $21.95. Limited.
Dawson City, Vol. 15, No. 2. $19.95.
Denali, Vol. 15, No. 3. $9.95.
The Kuskokwim River, Vol. 15, No. 4. $19.95.
Katmai Country, Vol. 16, No. 1. $19.95.
North Slope Now, Vol. 16, No. 2. $9.95.
The Tanana Basin, Vol. 16, No. 3. $9.95.
* The Copper Trail, Vol. 16, No. 4. $19.95.
* The Nushagak Basin, Vol. 17, No. 1. $19.95.
* Juneau, Vol. 17, No. 2. Out of print.
* The Middle Yukon River, Vol. 17, No. 3. $19.95.
* The Lower Yukon River, Vol. 17, No. 4. $19.95.
* Alaska's Weather, Vol. 18, No. 1. $9.95.
* Alaska's Volcanoes, Vol. 18, No. 2. $19.95.
* Admiralty Island: Fortress of Bears, Vol. 18, No. 3. Out of print.
* Unalaska/Dutch Harbor, Vol. 18, No. 4. $21.95. Limited.
* Skagway: A Legacy of Gold, Vol. 19, No. 1. $9.95.
Alaska: The Great Land, Vol. 19, No. 2. $9.95.
Kodiak, Vol. 19, No. 3. Out of print.
Alaska's Railroads, Vol. 19, No. 4. $19.95.
Prince William Sound, Vol. 20, No. 1. $9.95.
Southeast Alaska, Vol. 20, No. 2. $19.95.
Arctic National Wildlife Refuge, Vol. 20, No. 3. $19.95.
Alaska's Bears, Vol. 20, No. 4. $19.95.
The Alaska Peninsula, Vol. 21, No. 1. $19.95.
The Kenai Peninsula, Vol. 21, No. 2. $19.95.
People of Alaska, Vol. 21, No. 3. $19.95.
Prehistoric Alaska, Vol. 21, No. 4. $19.95.
Fairbanks, Vol. 22, No. 1. $19.95.
The Aleutian Islands, Vol. 22, No. 2. $19.95.
Rich Earth: Alaska's Mineral Industry, Vol. 22, No. 3. $19.95.
World War II in Alaska, Vol. 22, No. 4. $19.95.
Anchorage, Vol. 23, No. 1. $21.95.
Native Cultures in Alaska, Vol. 23, No. 2. $19.95.

The Brooks Range, Vol. 23, No. 3. $19.95.
Moose, Caribou and Muskox, Vol. 23, No. 4. $19.95.
Alaska's Southern Panhandle, Vol. 24, No. 1. $19.95.
The Golden Gamble, Vol. 24, No. 2. $19.95.
Commercial Fishing in Alaska, Vol. 24, No. 3. $19.95.
Alaska's Magnificent Eagles, Vol. 24, No. 4. $19.95.
Steve McCutcheon's Alaska, Vol. 25, No. 1. $21.95.
Yukon Territory, Vol. 25, No. 2. $21.95.
Climbing Alaska, Vol. 25, No. 3. $21.95.
Frontier Flight, Vol. 25, No. 4. $21.95.
Restoring Alaska: Legacy of an Oil Spill, Vol. 26, No. 1. $21.95.
World Heritage Wilderness, Vol. 26, No. 2. $21.95.
The Bering Sea, Vol. 26, No. 3. $21.95.
Russian America, Vol. 26, No. 4, $21.95
Best of ALASKA GEOGRAPHIC®, Vol. 27, No. 1, $24.95
Seals, Sea Lions and Sea Otters, Vol. 27, No. 2, $21.95
Painting Alaska, Vol. 27, No. 3, $21.95
Living Off the Land, Vol. 27, No. 4, $21.95

* Available in hardback (library binding) — $24.95 each.

PRICES AND AVAILABILITY SUBJECT TO CHANGE

Membership in The Alaska Geographic Society includes a subscription to *ALASKA GEOGRAPHIC*®, the Society's colorful, award-winning quarterly. Contact us for current membership rates or to request a free catalog.

The *ALASKA GEOGRAPHIC*® back issues listed above can be ordered directly from us. **NOTE:** This list was current in early 2001. If more than a year has elapsed since that time, contact us before ordering to check prices and availability of back issues, particularly for books marked "Limited."

When ordering back issues please add $5 for the first book and $2 for each additional book ordered for Priority Mail. Inquire for postage rates to non-U.S. addresses. To order, send check or money order (U.S. funds) or VISA or MasterCard information (including expiration date and your daytime phone number) with list of titles desired to:

ALASKA GEOGRAPHIC.

P.O. Box 93370 • Anchorage, AK 99509-3370
Phone (907) 562-0164 • Toll free (888) 255-6697
Fax (907) 562-0479 • e-mail: info@akgeo.com

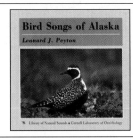
NEXT ISSUE: Vol. 28, No. 2

Glaciers of Alaska

Glaciers comprise some of Alaska's main topographical features. In this all-new issue, read about how ice moves mountains and how to recognize previously glaciated terrain; find the best places to see the state's glaciers close-up; and discover different types of glaciers and how they affect surrounding animal and plant life. Illustrated with stunning photos and informative maps. To members summer 2001.